A WORLDLY CHRISTIANITY

Down-To-Earth Sermons
On The Gospel Texts
(Series A)
Advent To Lent
And
Lent To Pentecost

PAUL P. KUENNING

Paul P. Kuenning
Fairway Press

A WORLDLY CHRISTIANITY

FIRST EDITION
Copyright © 1995 by
Paul P. Kuenning

Scripture quotations are from the *Revised Standard Version of the Bible*, copyrighted 1946, 1952 (c), 1971, 1973, by the Division of Christian Education of the National Council of the Churches of Christ in the USA. Used by permission.

Library of Congress Catalog Card Number: 95-94470

ISBN 0-7880-0614-2   PRINTED IN U.S.A.

DEDICATION

TO MARY JO
without whose encouragement, assistance
and love this book would not be.

Table Of Contents

Introduction

The title of this little book of homilies on the Gospel texts requires explanation. What is meant by a "Worldly Christianity"? Many would argue that the term is self-contradictory. According to a traditional interpretation, 'worldly', far from providing any sort of ideal description of Christianity, is unalterably opposed to it. It is a synonym for all that is non-Christian, wicked and evil. It's true that the Scriptures often describe the world as the kingdom and playground of the devil and Christians are admonished to keep themselves "unspotted from the world". (James 1:27) St. Paul describes the spirit of the world as opposed to the spirit of God (I Cor. 2:12) and St. James calls friendship with the world "enmity with God." (4:4) But these and like portions of Scripture deal only with a single viewpoint, and when taken by themselves, provide a one-sided interpretation.

The Biblical concept of the 'world' is not only one of sin and corruption, but of grace and redemption. Created by God, the world remains in its entirety under the Lordship of Christ. (Col. 1:15-20) It is in the world that God's Kingdom takes root and grows, (Mt. 13) and it is to the world that God expresses the divine Love in Jesus Christ. (John 3:16) That this love for the world is to be mediated by the faithful is made clear by Jesus words, "As thou didst send me into the world so I have sent them into the world." (John 17:18)

A Christian faith which can positively identify itself as 'worldly' is one that takes seriously the proclamation of Scripture that the manifestation of God's love in Christ and the resolution of our human destiny are totally immersed in this world. It is one which believes that the Incarnation of Jesus Christ unites the Word and the world.

I recall how a beloved Seminary professor counseled his students to prepare their sermons with a Bible in one hand and a newspaper in the other. This admonition to view the meaning of current events in the light of God's will was grounded in the refusal to put asunder that which God has joined together. A faith which sets itself off from the world and renounces its role as conscience, guide and directive for all of life, is not just lacking in relevance, it is devoid of reality. It falls into the category of a fanciful faith. It is an 'up-in-the-air' religion.

To emphasize the 'worldliness' of the Christian faith does not mean that humanity is idolized or that the centrality of God is compromised. It only means that the human arena, this life, this world, and this moment, is the only place and time we are given to experience and to utilize the power and love of God. Neither does the assertion of the Gospel's 'worldliness' compromise nor detract from the significance of the Biblical proclamation that faith alone justifies and redeems. It rather adds to it by describing more precisely the nature and function of that faith through which salvation is bestowed. It is a faith active in love. It is a faith opposed to hunger, homelessness, racism, unjust war and unnecessary violence. It is a faith which strives for human justice and the liberation of those who live under oppression. So long as faith is yoked to Christ it cannot be divorced from all that is human. And this includes the sphere of the political, for politics lies at the heart and center of our human life. It not only affects but frequently exercises a decisive influence upon the most critical moral issues and matters of life and death. For this reason a 'Worldly Christianity' does more than merely 'tolerate' the interpenetration of faith with politics and other mundane matters. It boldly asserts they belong together.

The tendency persists, however, to view the Christian life as a separate or special realm and to set it off in isolation from our earthly existence. It is ironic that the Church which attempts to follow a policy of political abstinence helps to create the very conditions by which it can be quietly and subtly coopted by the state. Since silence most often implies consent, an absence of action results in the identification of the Church with the oppressive actions of the state. It is not difficult to document the disastrous results of this 'malady of muteness'. An example which comes most quickly to mind is that of the Church in Germany under the regime of Hitler. Cases can also be cited which lie much closer to our own doorsteps. Throughout the war in Vietnam, the community of the Church in the U.S. remained for the most part silently supportive of a bloody and unprincipled militarism, while being kind and generous to its victims. As this war was raging, I attended the synodical convention of a major Protestant Church body. During the morning session the delegates received, with a standing ovation, a report that they had exceeded their goal of providing blankets for the homeless victims of the U.S. 'incursion' into Cambodia. But that same afternoon a recommendation to condemn the military action which created these refugees was soundly defeated.

This ominous affliction of silence was demonstrated again in the face of the bellicosity and ultra-patriotism which character- ized the U.S. invasions of Grenada and Panama, and the war against Iraq. The latter engagement was prosecuted with scarcely any res- ervations and the ferocious utilization of carpet bombing and guided missiles produced the most efficient killing machine in military history. Yet it was a war with hardly any moral justification, and one that might have been avoided had there been sufficient opposi- tion to it. In the aftermath of this tragic conflict the Church and its people once more responded with commendable charity and con- cern for those who suffered its ravages. Again we were provided with a disastrous demonstration of the fact that the Christian com- munity cannot evade its political responsibilities by fulfilling its vocation of personal compassion.

This problem is by no means confined to the question of militarism and war. On the domestic front, the Church has for the most part responded to the heart-rending growth of homelessness and poverty with a strong accent on charitable endeavor, providing additional food pantries and places of refuge for those forced to live in the streets. Any kind of lasting solution to the root causes of these problems, however, must necessarily include advocacy as well as charity.

Where churches have taken an activist stance, it is often curiously devoid of a practical humanitarian concern or a well- grounded Biblical support. The current call for a so-called 'tough love' is a case in point. It has expressed itself politically in a will- ingness to 'balance the budget' on the backs of the poor. It makes victims of the most vulnerable. Funding for programs designed to help those struggling to survive, such as Aid to Dependent Chil- dren, food stamps, job training and child care are cut, while at the same time huge tax breaks are designed to benefit the wealthy and billions of dollars are allocated for unnecessary and destructive weapons of war. This is a recipe for social disaster, and it flies directly in the face of the fundamental Biblical injunction to give priority concern to the needs of the poor. Likewise, the push for more prisons, stiffer sentences and capital punishment, not only fails to reflect the teachings of Christ, but provides no practical solutions to the real dilemmas of crime, violence and drugs. Until government responds more adequately to crucial concerns such as unemployment and underemployment, unjust tax structures, lack of adequate housing and medical care for all people, these problems will continue to grow.

When the church engages in private volunteerism without political advocacy it acts like persons who frantically place pans and buckets around to catch the rain seeping into their home. At some point it is necessary to repair the roof. The critical question posed over a half century ago by the German theologian and martyr, Dietrich Bonhoeffer, still awaits a definitive answer, "Has the church merely to gather up those whom the wheel has crushed, or has she to prevent the wheel from crushing them?"

The sermons which follow seek to show how the Gospel of Jesus Christ carries its powerful message of life and hope into every nook and cranny of our earthly existence. They give expressions to the ways in which this Gospel not only provides the motivating spirit for acts of personal compassion but instills the impetus for the entire body of Christ to enter into the struggle for justice on every level, including the social and political. In a word, they open a window in which to view the Scripture's vision of "A Worldly Christianity".

1st Sunday In Advent

Living In Readiness

Matthew 24:37-44

> *"As were the days of Noah, so will be the coming of
> the Son of man. For as in those days before the flood
> they were eating and drinking, marrying and giving in
> marriage, until the day when Noah entered the ark, and
> they did not know until the flood came and swept them
> all away, so will be the coming of the Son of man. Then
> two men will be in the field; one is taken and one is left.
> Two women will be grinding at the mill; one is taken
> and one is left. Watch therefore, for you do not know
> on what day your Lord is coming. But know this, that if
> the householder had known in what part of the night
> the thief was coming, he would have watched and would
> not have let his house be broken into. Therefore you
> also must be ready; for the son of man is coming at an
> hour you do not expect."*

The entire 24th and 25th chapters of the Gospel of Matthew are devoted to a series of exhortations and parables in which Jesus calls upon his followers to be constantly prepared for the sudden arrival of the Day of the Lord, when the Son of Man will come to earth again and establish God's Kingdom in its fullness.

Whatever one may think or believe about this teaching in its original and literal form, it contains the essence of a truth which is timeless, universal and eminently practical. It is the call to live as those who are prepared and ready for unexpected events and an unforeseeable future.

How often we get the feeling that we would like to peek into the future and know with certainty what fate holds in store for us. In this pervasive desire lies the reason for the age-old attraction of astrology and the 'fortune teller' or the seer. Perhaps in the stars, or in the myriad lines that crease our palm, or in the mystical vision of a 'prophetic spirit' we can learn just what lies ahead and discover the means to benefit from it, evade it, or prepare ourselves to face it. But the haunting hope will never be realized, and it may be far better that way. It is hard enough to face the difficulties and hardships of life as they arise, without knowing years ahead the inevitability of their coming. And as for joys, the quality of surprise enriches the pleasures they bring.

In this human life, the future, for better or worse, remains for the most part hidden. Even Jesus, speaking in our text about the inevitability of the end of this world and the coming judgment, admitted he lacked any knowledge of its timing. "But of that day or that hour no one knows," he said, "not even the angels in heaven, nor the Son, but only the Father".(Mark 13:32)

There is just one thing about the future that we really know for sure. Eventually everything in this world will end, including our own lives. We know for certain we will die, but we don't know the way nor the day nor the hour.

When I was a youngster growing up in Nebraska, our family used to listen to a lot of country music on the radio. Among our favorite singers was Hank Williams, and one of his songs was called, "We're Getting Closer to the Grave Each Day." Not exactly an uplifting thought in and by itself, but the last lines went like this, "So every day you live, love and forgive. We're getting closer to the grave each day." Every day you live, love and forgive. These words contain the key to the practical meaning of Jesus' advice to live as those who are ready. To live in readiness for whatever may come and for that which eventually must come, is to make the most of each moment and each day that we live.

In his little booklet entitled Peace Is Every Step, the Buddhist monk, Thich Nhat Hanh, reminds us of what a glorious gift it is to simply breathe and smile and become aware of the beautiful things around us and the resources within us. The past is behind, the future is beyond, the present moment is all we have to realize happiness, to find peace, to serve others, and to prepare for what lies ahead. He puts it this way, "Our appointment with life is in the present moment. If we do not have peace and joy right now, when will we have peace and joy, tomorrow, or after tomorrow? What is preventing us from realizing happiness right now in this wonder ful, present moment?"

Living in readiness, being ready for whatever comes, involves a concentration on the 'now'. It means living in the present, utilizing it to the fullest, enjoying its gifts, wrestling with its problems, dealing with its difficulties, realizing its possibilities and seizing its opportunities. This is also what Jesus means when he asks his followers to 'watch'. Watching is not just standing and looking and waiting for something to happen or for someone to arrive. It means being alert, alive, and awake. It means living with our eyes and our minds and our hearts open wide to the wonders that surround us and to the tasks which beckons us. To watch is to live as those who are fully awake to the potential of the present moment.

Physically speaking, of course, we cannot always be awake. Our bodies find rest and refreshment in sleep, and our minds find relief from the daily cares and anxieties. As Shakespeare described it, "Sleep that soothes the raveled sleeve of care", is a necessity and a blessing. But there is another kind of sleep which is dangerous and may even be deadly. It is a 'sleep' which allows us to remain insensitive to the realities of the world around us, to the possibilities and challenges of the present moment. It is a 'sleep' which closes our eyes to the beauty of the sky and the stars, the flowers and the trees, and to the needs of the people around us.

A little book put out by the Alanon group contains this precious bit of philosophy: "God gives us just one day at a time, today, to live. By doing our best today, we will have no regrets or fears. We can do something for this twenty-four hours that would be impossible if we thought we had to do it for a life-time."

Some time ago a good friend told me of a precious experience he had with his two children. He took them for a drive in the country and arrived at a very beautiful spot near a softly flowing river lined with trees. The day was sunny and bright. Suddenly he was seized with a desire to tell them how very much he loved and cared for them. In his own words and his own way he did just that. And he said it brought him a great emotional release. His fears were quieted and he experienced a peace he had not felt before.

This little story illustrates an important truth. Expressing our love today, not only helps to erase guilt over the past, but fear

13

of the future. When Jesus tells us to 'watch' and to be 'ready' he is in reality telling us to stay awake and alert, to use the present moment as the only time we really have to live and to love and to follow in his steps.

The Fruit of Repentance

Matthew 3:1-12

> *In those days came John the Baptist, preaching in the wilderness of Judea, "Repent, for the kingdom of heaven is at hand." For this is he who was spoken of by the prophet Isaiah when he said,*
>
> *"The voice of one crying in the wilderness: Prepare the way of the Lord, make his paths straight." Now John wore a garment of camel's hair, and a leather girdle around his waist; and his food was locusts and wild honey. Then went out to him Jerusalem and all Judea and all the region about the Jordan, and they were baptized by him in the river Jordan, confessing their sins.*
>
> *But when he saw many of the Pharisees and Sadducees coming for baptism, he said to them, "You brood of vipers! Who warned you to flee from the wrath to come? Bear fruit that befits repentance, and do not presume to say to yourselves, 'We have Abraham as our father'; for I tell you, God is able from these stones to raise up children to Abraham. Even now the axe is laid to the root of the trees; every tree therefore that does not bear good fruit is cut down and thrown into the fire."*
>
> *"I baptize you with water for repentance, but he who is coming after me is mightier than I, whose sandals I am not worthy to carry; he will baptize you with the Holy Spirit and with fire. His winnowing fork is in his hand, and he will clear his threshing floor and gather his wheat into the granary, but the chaff he will burn with unquenchable fire."*

John the Baptist appeared one day out in the desolate Judean countryside on the banks of the Jordan River, calling on people to repent of their sins and proclaiming the good news that the Kingdom of God was at hand.

15

That prophetic voice has not been stilled, and will never be. It comes to us again in this Advent season. It cannot be heard in the Christmas carols that blare out from the loudspeakers in the department stores where we frantically search out gifts for the person 'who has everything'. Neither is it communicated in the myriad of T.V. Christmas programs with their popular, soft and sentimental music and message, blending "Silent Night" with "Chestnuts Roasting on an Open Fire" and "Rudolph the Red-Nosed Reindeer". The prophetic voice still echoes forth from the wilderness, from desolate and unexpected places. It may be heard in the quiet closet of prayer, in the still small voice that whispers its word in moments of self-examination and meditation, in the reading of Scripture, or in the earnest conversation with friends about things that matter most.

And this prophetic word is always as tough as truth, yet pregnant with promise. It is not an easy word, willing to let us off the hook of our nagging guilt on the basis of a perfunctory act of worship or a gift painlessly given. It is similar in this way to the word John the Baptist spoke to the Pharisees and Sadducees when they came to him for baptism. "You brood of vipers," he said, "Bear fruit that befits repentance and do not presume to say to yourselves, 'We have Abraham as our father.'"

The prophetic word is hard as steel. It is, as Jeremiah put it, "like a hammer that breaks the rock in pieces". (Jer. 23:29) It crushes with a single blow the sham and pretense, the false pride behind which we hide our emptiness and our desperate need. "Do not presume to say to yourselves, 'We have Abraham as our father' ". In one fell swoop the prophetic word sweeps aside the false sense of security which we place upon our particular race or religion or nationality. With one stroke of the hammer it smashes to pieces reliance upon wealth or possessions, ancestry or worldly status, and leaves them exposed for the heap of rubble and trash that they really are.

But the prophetic word is far more than a warning of what not to do. It is also a positive word. It is a word of promise and of hope. It gives us direction. It tells us what must be done to open our hearts to the coming of God's Kingdom and Love. The word is

16

short and simple, yet the universe can scarcely contain the extent of its meaning. "Bear fruit that befits repentance." What a mouthful! What an earful! Repentance is more than just a thought, more than a feeling of sorrow. Repentance is nothing unless it involves action, unless it bears fruit.

Many a time I've told my parents or wife or children that I was sorry for what I had done, for things which hurt or distressed them. It would have been just as well had I said nothing at all, for the test of my sorrow, the content of my repentance, would be demonstrated only by doing those things which furthered their happiness and well-being. Sorrow over sins can only be made manifest in acts of love. The root meaning of the Greek word translated as "repent" in our text is to 'turn around' or to 'change direction'. It describes not just a mental and attitudinal alteration, but an actual, tangible movement toward a new way of life.

Are you really sorry today for the way you treated someone yesterday, for the mean or malicious act, for the pain you intentionally inflicted on someone unable to defend themselves? Are you sorry today for the kindness you intended to extend but never did, the worthwhile cause you wanted to support, but failed to follow through? Then bear the fruit that makes repentance real. Turn around, and act differently. God's Word directs us, God's help assists us, God's love inspires us.

But John said that the Lord would not only bring the fire of the Spirit to aid us in our endeavor, but also the fire of judgment. "He will clear his threshing floor and gather his wheat into the granary, but the chaff, he will burn with unquenchable fire." Are we willing to direct that judgment upon our own lives now, before the final day? Are we willing to sort out some of the waste and the rubbish that fills up so much of our daily existence, and toss it aside? Can we act to divide the wheat from the chaff this side of the Judgment Day? What are the things in your life and mine that are not only worthless, and wasteful, but even destructive? Wrap them in a little package, tie it with a bow and throw it in the garbage to be carted off to the incinerator. Sorting out and discarding the habits and the behavior which retard and stifle positive growth and change results in bearing good fruit.

And what is the fruit of true repentance? One of John's forerunners, the prophet Isaiah spelled it out in specific terms for the people of Judah in his day: "Cease to do evil, learn to do good; seek justice, correct oppression; defend the fatherless, plead for the widow". "Then it will be," he said, "that though your sins are like scarlet, they shall be as white as snow...";(Is.1:17-18) a truth summed up by a New Testament Prophet in the words, "Love covers a multitude of sins."(I Peter 4:8)

But perhaps no one captured more concisely the essence of this truth than John the Baptist himself. As St. Luke relates this same incident he tell us that when John called on the people to bear the fruit of repentance, and they asked him what to do, he did not equivocate or generalize, but replied, "He who has two coats, let him share with him who has none, and he who has food, let him do likewise."(Luke 3:11)

His word to us is just as plain, just as difficult, and just as true today as it was then!

Preaching Good News to the Poor

Matt. 11:2-6

> *Now when John heard in prison about the deeds of the Christ, he sent word by his disciples and said to him, "Are you he who is to come, or shall we look for another?" And Jesus answered them, "Go and tell John what you hear and see: the blind receive their sight and the dead are raised up, and the poor have good news preached to them. And blessed is he who takes no offense at me."*

John the Baptist was in jail. He was there because he had the temerity to warn the ruler of Galilee, King Herod, that it was unlawful for him to live with Herodias, the wife of his brother. Herod, egged on by Herodias, had John seized and thrown into prison.

Prophets like John the Baptist, who refuse to dress in the cashmere coats and the button-down suits of the establishment, who refuse to bend according to whichever way the winds of popularity may be blowing, and who insist on speaking the truth regardless of the consequences, often end up as jail-birds. Prophets like John are perceived by the powerful rich, who live in luxury while they rob and oppress the poor, as enemies. It is the fate of prophets to be rejected, persecuted, imprisoned or even killed.

In El Salvador six priests were dragged from their beds and shot, their bodies left bloody and mutilated in the yard of the University where they taught. Why? Because they had dared to stand up for the rights of the poor and because this passion for justice was construed as an act of sedition against the ruling powers. A colleague of these martyred priests, said later that to speak the truth about his country at that time was to place one's life in jeopardy. To one degree or another, that is true anytime and everywhere. It is true in our own country and in our own churches. To speak the truth is to provoke opposition, to stir up controversy, to

19

invite persecution of one kind or another. That is why truth is so seldom spoken. That is why there are always very few prophets.

The text says that while John the Baptist was in prison, he heard about the things that Jesus was doing and that he sent some of his followers to ask Jesus if he was really the Messiah. They were instructed to inquire if he was the promised Savior whom the Scriptures proclaimed would one day come to bring into being the Kingdom of God. Jesus answered John's disciples in this way, "Go and tell John what you hear and see: the blind receive their sight and the lame walk, lepers are cleansed and the deaf hear, and the dead are raised up, and the poor have good news preached to them."

The first part of Jesus answer should not be overlooked. "Go and tell John what you hear <u>and</u> <u>see</u>." The coming of God's Kingdom in the ministry of Jesus was not a matter of proclamation only, but also of demonstration. Tell John what you hear <u>and</u> what you <u>see</u> happening. It is reminiscent of a comment once made by the Apostle Philip. After Jesus called Philip to be his disciple, Philip went and told his friend Nathaniel that he had found the promised Messiah. Nathaniel was hesitant to believe that this could possibly be true and referring to the lowly village in which Jesus had been reared he said, "Can any good thing come out of Nazareth?" To which Philip replied, "Come and see."

It is much more convincing to actually see something than only hear about it. As James Whitcomb Riley once put it, "I'd rather see a sermon than hear one any day." Teachers have found that an interesting way for small children to learn is in what is called a "Show and Tell" time. The children bring something to show their classmates and then tell the others about it, or explain it to them. The point to note here is that telling someone about something becomes much more understandable after you have first shown it to them. A real Christian witness never settles for only one half of the equation. The signs of God's Kingdom to which Jesus pointed were things that were being daily demonstrated in his life. The lame, the deaf and blind were being healed, and lepers were being cleansed. Preaching good news to the poor is always an act as well as a word. It is reaching out in deeds of compassion to the ill and the aged to the handicapped, the disabled, the forgotten and the neglected.

It is important to note in this connection that Jesus includes among the activities of his ministry, the cleansing of lepers. Leprosy in Jesus day was a dreaded disease. People exaggerated its contagion. Lepers were almost completely ostracized. They were the outcasts of society. But Jesus was willing to touch the untouchables, to reach out to the rejected. That is still the way the good news is preached today, in ministries of compassion and advocacy for the victims of AIDS, for the mentally ill, for the victims of Alzheimers and other crippling diseases of the aging, to those persons we tend to turn our back upon, because of our own dread or fear.

Jesus concluded the description of his ministry with these words..."the dead are raised up and the poor have good news preached to them". Those who had died both physically and spiritually, both literally and figuratively, were receiving new life and new hope. But the best is saved to last. "The poor have good news preached to them." Is there still any good news to proclaim to the poor? It can be found among other places in the struggle for justice, for jobs, for decent housing and health care, in any and every effort to alleviate the shame and suffering of poverty. To preach that kind of good news to the poor means more than talking the talk. It means walking the walk. It means, as the prophet Isaiah said, to strengthen "the weak hands, and the knees that tremble".(Is.35:3) It means, as Jesse Jackson has said, to keep "hope alive!" It is not an easy task to preach good news to the poor. It is in fact a hard, difficult, demanding one. From the human point of view alone, the challenge is overwhelming, if not impossible. But we are only called to do what we can, in thanks for what God has done for us. We cannot do more than that, but neither can we do less. As Christians we will never do less. For as Christians we believe in the coming of God's Kingdom in Christ and in its partial realization here and now in this life through the likes of you and me, not just in some other world or some other life or through someone else.

We have faith that God's Kingdom can and will be established in this world, and that it is God's intention to use you and me to bring it about. Our faith enables us to believe again in the power of goodness to transform lives, to keep on believing, to hope against hope, that the world can be changed, that God's Kingdom will come on earth as in heaven. That is why Jesus, after praising John the Baptist, added that the person who "is least in the Kingdom of heaven is greater than he". It is when we take on the characteristic of a little child whose faith and hope is not yet tarnished by failure or crippled by cynicism, that we enter into God's Kingdom and with our lives become the preachers of its good news to the poor. For as Jesus said, using a little child as an example, it is those who are the least, the humblest, the most child-like, who are in reality the greatest.(Luke (9:47-48)

The good news which we preach to the poor will not always meet with success. It will not always bear fruit or establish God's Kingdom in our midst. Sometimes there will be no tangible effect at all. But the 'greatness' of what we do lies not in the results but in the doing. As T.S. Eliot once wrote "For us there is only the trying, the rest is not our business". Our faith will never let us do less than try. Then and only then, with a good conscience, can we leave the rest to God.

God With Us

Matthew 1:18-25

> *Now the birth of Jesus Christ took place in this way. When his mother Mary had been betrothed to Joseph, before they came together she was found to be with child of the Holy Spirit; and her husband Joseph, being a just man and unwilling to put her to shame, resolved to divorce her quietly. But as he considered this, behold, an angel of the Lord appeared to him in a dream, saying, "Joseph, son of David, do not fear to take Mary your wife, for that which is conceived in her is of the Holy Spirit; she will bear a son, and you shall call his name Jesus, for he will save his people from their sins." All this took place to fulfil what the Lord had spoken by the prophet; "Behold, a virgin shall conceive and bear a son, and his name shall be called Emmanuel" (which means, God with us). When Joseph woke from sleep, he did as the angel of the Lord commanded him; he took his wife, but knew her not until she had borne a son; and he called his name Jesus.*

In this story of Jesus' birth, as in many other parts of the Scripture, the human and the divine are merged in a remarkable manner. What is limited, finite and destined to die is united with what is unlimited, infinite and eternal.

When Joseph realized that Mary was going to have a child and knew that he was not the father, his immediate and quite understandable reaction was one of mistrust and accusaton. His ego was bruised and he feared the disapproval of his family and friends. He decided to quietly break off their betrothal so as to spare both Mary and himself as much shame and embarrassment as possible. But in the midst of this very human reaction, Joseph had a dream,and in that dream he received an astonishing revelation. The message he perceived was that out of this seemingly scandalous situation, a

23

marvelous and miraculous thing was about to take place.

Like Joseph, our vision too is limited and restricted by our humanity. It is difficult to see beyond the surface of things. We tend to judge and condemn others by outward appearances. We are inclined to draw cynical conclusions, quick to lose hope that things can change for the better, or that any good thing can come out of what appears to be evil. But like Joseph, we also carry within us that spark of divinity which enables us to dream dreams and see visions, to catch a glimpse of life's mystery and possibilities. There lies within us the capacity to conjure up the dream of a world where suspicion, mistrust, fear, hate and prejudice give way to those of love and trust, peace and community. It is important for us to nourish this ability to dream, and to hope and believe that things can be better than they are, that 'miracles' are still possible. If we allow it to wither away, if it is extinguished through lack of faith, then to a great extent our life is impoverished and diminished. As the writer of the Proverbs said, "Where there is no vision, the people perish."(Proverbs 29:18)

It was that 20th century martyr and prophet, Martin Luther King, Jr., who articulated most accurately the dream of what the building of God's Kingdom in our own society involves. He had the vision of a mighty crusade to break down the dividing walls of racial hostility and prejudice. He saw the day coming when persons of all races and creeds and religions would accept one another and live together as brothers and sisters in peace and harmony. And his life was a witness to the power of that dream to motivate and activate human endeavor.

Joseph's dream also contained not only a personal consolation but a vision of life and hope for all people. The heart of that hope was contained in the angel's message that Mary's baby would grow up to fulfill the prophecy of Isaiah, " 'Behold a virgin shall conceive and bear a son, and his name shall be called Emmanuel'(which means God with us)."

We celebrate the birth of Jesus because the Nativity story conveys the vision of a Creator God who is not far away, who dwells in our midst and who shares our humanity. "Emmanuel, God with us". That is the deepest meaning of Christmas and the

Incarnation. God is not to be found in some transcendental concept, or theological formulation, or esoteric liturgy, but in the flesh and blood reality of our living and our dying. God is not up in the air, but down on the earth. And this truth has tremendous significance for our living. It means above all that it is this earth and not heaven that constitutes the heart of our existence. It is here that the Love of God is to be experienced and shared. It means that this life and not the life beyond has the greatest significance for now. It means that this real actual world of suffering and death and disease, of politics and economics and business, of marriage and child-rearing, and personal relationships, is where we will find and serve God, or we will do it nowhere. In John Steinbeck's Grapes of Wrath, the 'former preacher', Jim Casy, voices his questions about the reality of a religion that is fixed on heaven and forgets the earth. "Hope of heaven", he says, "when their lives aren't lived? Holy Sperit when their own sperit is downcast an' sad? They got to live before they can afford to die." In the real meaning of Christmas lies an answer to this searing criticism of a religion that has lost touch with the earth. Christianity is not something supernatural and holy in terms of being removed or detached from this life and its deficiencies and problems. It is rather something which lives only in the midst of the world and in the heart of humanity, it is God "with us."

In Ernest Feil's book, The Theology of Dietrich Bonhoeffer, these words of the martyred German Lutheran pastor are quoted, "They who evade the earth do not find God. ... They find a world beyond to be sure, but one that is not God's world. They who evade the earth in order to find God, find only themselves." Here Bonhoeffer expressed in a pungent and profound way, the true meaning of the Incarnation as Emmanuel, God with us. We look for God in some mystical place or transcendental experience. But that is exactly where we make our mistake. That is why only a few lowly shepherds who followed their vision to a common cow shed and a crude manger bed, discovered the infant Jesus. So we continue to search for God in the wrong places, not hearing the word of Isaiah that was relayed to Joseph in a dream, "Emmanuel-God with us."

An incident that occurred during the first years of my parish ministry comes to my mind. I had just put on my ministerial robe, surplice, and stole, and was preparing to walk to the sacristy to begin the service, when a mother with a small boy about three years old approached me. It was his first time in the church. The little boy stopped and looked up at me. His eyes widened in wonderment at my auspicious apparel, and in a hushed voice he said, "Mommie, is that God?" In my embarrassment I hastily tried to set him straight. But his question sometimes haunts me still. Where shall we point those who like that little boy and myself search for the presence of God, who look for signs of divinity in this very finite world? We can point to our fellow human beings, to the neighbor who is in need, to the poor, the homeless, the disabled, the sick, the destitute, the aged, the lonely, the mentally ill, to those whose lives mirror the divinity of their Creator.

To find God and to serve God in the world in which we live and in the midst of the humanity by which we are surrounded and of which we are a part, that is to realize the deepest meaning of Christmas. It is also to discover the deepest meaning of our own lives.

1st Sunday After Christmas

Herod, Then and Now

Matt. 2: 13-23

> *Now when they had departed, behold, an angel of the Lord appeared to Joseph in a dream and said, "Rise, take the child and his mother, and flee to Egypt, and remain there till I tell you; for Herod is about to search for the child, to destroy him." And he rose and took the child and his mother by night, and departed to Egypt, and remained there until the death of Herod. This was to fulfill what the Lord had spoken by the prophet, "Out of Egypt have I called my son." Then Herod, when he saw that he had been tricked by the wise men, was in a furious rage, and he sent and killed all the male children in Bethlehem and in all that region who were two years old or under, according to the time which he had ascertained from the wise men. Then was fulfilled what was spoken by the prophet Jeremiah:*
>
> *" A voice was heard in Ramah, wailing and loud lamentation, Rachel weeping for her children; she refused to be consoled, because they were no more." But when Herod died, behold, an angel of the Lord appeared in a dream to Joseph in Egypt, saying, "Rise, take the child and his mother, and go to the land of Israel, for those who sought the child's life are dead." And he rose and took the child and his mother, and went to the land of Israel. But when he heard that Archelaus reigned over Judea in place of his father Herod, he was afraid to go there, and being warned in a dream he withdrew to the district of Galilee. And he went and dwelt in a city called Nazareth, that what was spoken by the prophets might be fulfilled, "He shall be called a Nazarene."*

The flight of the Holy Family to Egypt has sometimes been portrayed in a quiet, peaceful, pastoral manner. Joseph leads a donkey on which Mary sits cradling the infant Jesus. It is an almost idyllic scene. In reality, it was a hurried, furtive and fearful departure, a dash for life. It took place in the dead of night, as they fled from the terrible wrath of a tyrant determined to kill their child.

The man who became known as Herod the Great had been appointed governor of Judea under Roman authority about 47 B.C. Several years later he had taken the title of king. In the early years of his reign he completed a number of beneficial projects, among them the building of the Temple in Jerusalem. He had also shown a capacity for generosity as when he remitted taxes in a time of famine to ease the burden of the people. But as history indicates, power retained and consolidated over a period of time, often leads to greed and corruption. Such was the case with Herod. During his later years he developed a psychotic hatred of anyone who might pose a challenge to his personal authority. When he became suspicious that members of his own family were plotting against him, he had his wife, mother-in-law, and three of his sons all assassinated.

It is not difficult to imagine the panic and fear which flooded the mind of this aging ruler when word came to him that a child had recently been born about whom there existed prophecies that he was to become the future king of the Jews. Herod had received this alarming news from three visitors to Jerusalem who had traveled hundreds of miles from the East, probably from the region we know today as Iran, Iraq or Saudi Arabia. They had followed some celestial apparition, a new star, or comet, possibly a conjunction of planets, which they believed to signal a fortuitous birth. These travelers were called Magi, a word sometimes rendered in English as "wise-men." They were skilled in astrology and the interpretation of dreams, also learned in the arts of philosophy, medicine and natural science. Many of these Magi had become counselors and teachers of the Persian kings. They had a reputation of being good and holy men, searchers after truth. What a contrast between the power-hungry, self-centeredness of King Herod, and the selflessness of these learned men who came bearing gifts for one they believed was destined to be a benevolent and righteous ruler.

Herod was determined to eliminate his potential rival as quickly as possible. He called together the religious leaders of Jerusalem and discovered there was a prophecy that the looked for Messiah-King would be born in Bethlehem. He then directed the Magi to go to Bethlehem and to bring him back word as to the child's whereabouts, adding the bold-face lie that it was his intention to go also and pay his respects. Later when Herod learned that the Magi had deceived him and returned to their home home by another route, the text says that he flew into a "furious rage". He estimated the earliest possible time that the birth of the child might have occurred. Then he issued the diabolical order for his soldiers to kill all the male children in Bethlehem and the surrounding region who were "two years old and under".

This massacre of small children and infants, whom the Church remembers as the Holy Innocents, is one of the most horrible and heart-rending events recorded in the New Testament. Matthew says that Jeremiah's prophesy was on that day fulfilled, "A voice was heard in Ramah, wailing and loud lamentation. Rachel weeping for her children" and refusing to be consoled, "because they were no more."

But Herod's primary target had eluded the ghastly sweep of his soldier's swords. Joseph had been warned in a dream to flee. Under cover of darkness the holy family headed for the closest border to the South. They arrived safely in Egypt, and remained there until King Herod died. Before Jesus was two years old he had joined the countless numbers who had gone before him and who would follow after, as refugees in a strange land, victims of a government that had become the assailant rather than the guardian of its people.

This poignant story of the flight into Egypt and the terrible tragedy which triggered it, reveals in the figure of Herod the King, the sad story, repeated throughout history, of the murderous misuse of the state's awesome authority and power. When Herod's political position appeared threatened, he ordered his soldiers to massacre little children, and they obeyed without question and killed without mercy. That is the duty of soldiers. It is what they are trained to do, and pledge themselves to do, when those in command deem it necessary. Today these soldiers are armed not with knives and swords but with powerful guns, with tanks and aircraft and with bombs and missiles, nuclear and otherwise. War waged with modern weapons is always an unmitigated disaster, and it always involves a slaughter of the innocents. In the war which the U.S. waged against Iraq about half of the thousands of casualties, dead and wounded, were civilians. Following the devastation wrought by the bombing the death rate for the children of Iraq rose three to four times its normal rate, due to the lack of pure water, food and medicines.

Wars and the preparation for wars continue to be the single greatest factor which rob innocent people and children of their birthright to the full and abundant life which their Creator desires them to have. Wars not only kill directly, but indirectly, for they consume trillions of dollars that could be used to alleviate and in some cases nearly eliminate the demons of poverty, hunger, homelessness, disease and illiteracy, which every day exact their terrible toll. This proclivity toward evil resides in the fact that the state is inclined to protect the power, prestige, wealth and self-interest of those who hold political office, regardless of the cost to those who as impoverished outsiders exist as a threat to this establishment.

Snatched from the clutches of Herod while still a little child, Jesus lived to teach us that obedience to any earthly power must always remain subservient to a greater allegiance. He made this clear when he called upon his followers to "seek first God's Kingdom and his righteousness." His oft-quoted dictum, "Render unto Caesar what belongs to Caesar and unto God what belongs to God," has to be understood in the light of those first words, namely that what belongs to God always has the priority. This does not mean that our allegiance to God's Kingdom involves automatic opposition to the state. In St. Paul's description of the "governing authorities" in the 13th chapter of his letter to the Romans, he describes them as "instituted by God". He calls on every person to obey governmental authority and says that to resist is to oppose "what God has appointed." This passage has, however, been frequently abbreviated and perverted in an attempt to justify the Christians obedience to a "Herod-like" government. St.Paul describes a civil authority which takes seriously its responsibility to provide for the real welfare of its people. This is made crystal clear. "Rulers are not a terror to good conduct, but to bad...Then do what is good and you will receive..approval." Finally the ruler is described as "the servant of God." St. Paul's description did not have in mind Herod, then or now.

In the book of Acts we are told that when Jesus disciples realized some laws of Herod were directly opposed to commands of their Lord, they declared "We must obey God rather than men."(Acts 5:29) And later still, when the Roman Empire continued the tradition of Herod by instituting a bloody persecution of Christians, St. John in his Apocalypse described that Empire and its rulers as a monster to be slain.(Rev. 13) The state, with its awesome power, can be a force for justice and peace, or for violence and oppression. It can be kind or cruel, godly or ungodly, the servant of God, or a beast to be destroyed.

It is vital that the Church and the individual Christian never subscribe to that false and blasphemous patriotism which cries,"My country right or wrong," and that in the pledge of allegiance to the flag of the nation, the words "under God" are stressed and understood. The misuse of governmental power and the perversion of justice by the State has left its winding, bloody trail of death and tears and human suffering from the time of Herod to the present. In our own country, within a single life span we have beheld the long, costly, frustrating and unfinished struggle for racial equality and equal opportunity. We have endured the senseless suffering, bloodshed and violence of Vietnam, Grenada, Panama, and Iraq, with their slaughter of the innocents. We have watched with sadness the growing hordes of the homeless poor and the mentally ill, of the aging without adequate health care, of children denied the education they deserve and require. We have witnessed the growth of state and national policies persecuting the poor and protecting the privileged, placing the priority on property rather than people, on a military defense against a projected foreign foe, rather than on the defense of its own people against the real and present enemies of hunger and disease, poverty and crime. Against all such evils the church and Christian believers are bound to resist in the name of God, proclaiming with the disciples of old, "We must obey God rather than men."

We can rejoice today, that even as Herod continues to raise his bloody arm of repression and violence in many areas throughout our world, the church has often persisted in the quest for justice and peace. It has continued at times to provide a rallying place and leadership for those who have stood up against a state which has deserted its God-given vocation. That is as it should be. As the South-African Archbishop Tutu has said, "Our faith compels us to speak up for justice and truth everywhere ... Denouncing injustice is for us a religious duty and not a political act."

The callous cruelty and lust for power of a Herod who drove Jesus parents into exile and massacred innocent children, is not dead. But neither is the living presence of God's love in Jesus Christ. It is that presence and spirit of love which enables us to serve as the conscience of the State, which keeps us alert and ever willing to resist and to reform the evil perpetrated by the Herods of our day.

1st Sunday After the Epiphany
The Baptism of Our Lord

Jesus' Baptism and Ours

Matthew 3: 13-17

> *Then Jesus came from Galilee to the Jordan to John, to be baptized by him. John would have prevented him, saying, "I need to be baptized by you, and do you come to me?" But Jesus answered him, "Let it be so now; for thus it is fitting for us to fulfill all righteousness." Then he consented. And when Jesus was baptized, he went up immediately from the water, and behold, the heavens were opened and he saw the Spirit of God descending like a dove, and alighting on him; and lo, a voice from heaven, saying, "This is my beloved Son, with whom I am well pleased."*

The event recorded in this text, raises an obvious question. Why did Jesus desire to receive baptism by John? If, as John proclaimed, his baptism signified repentance and the washing away of sin, why did one who was 'without sin' need it or want it?

The Baptizer recognized the problem, and at first refused Jesus request. Matthew writes, "John would have prevented him, saying, 'I need to be baptized by you, and do you come to me?'" Jesus reply is respectful but resolute. "Let it be so now; for thus it is fitting for us to fulfill all righteousness." What do these words mean? Somehow Jesus saw this act as a revelation of goodness and justice and love, which was his primary purpose in life. Since John was a baptizer of sinners, by receiving this baptism Jesus was voluntarily identifying himself fully with human kind. He was openly proclaiming himself as a brother of the sinful, the downtrodden and the outcast. He was announcing his solidarity with human suffering, pain and loneliness, with its frailty and failure and fear. Jesus was in effect saying that his role was not to set himself apart as a sinless critic and judge, but to share life with us as a fullfledged member of the human family. If his baptism, like his association with tax collectors and prostitutes, created misunderstanding and criticism, then let it be. He would not be sidetracked from his purpose in life. He had come to reveal God's righteousness, and his submission to John's baptism was a clear sign of that aim.

In the light of this understanding there is comfort and consolation to be found in Jesus' baptism. It means that in all of the trials and terrors and temptations of our lives, the love of God, and the spirit of Jesus will be there with us, "closer than breathing, nearer than hands or feet." Even when we walk through the valley of the shadow, we need not walk alone, for it is true, as he promised, "Lo I am with you always, even to the end of the age." All this is implicit in His baptism. It indicates the identification of the Creator with the creation, and as such it can be a source of solace and inner strength throughout all our life.

But if Jesus baptism symbolizes his empathy with us, then our baptism is the sign of our identification with him, and with the spirit of love and justice and peace which His life personified. The comfort of Jesus' baptism cannot be separated from the challenge implicit in our own. It will not do to accept the comfort and ignore the challenge. They are parts of a whole. Our baptism identifies us with the righteousness that Jesus' baptism exemplified. It challenges us to die daily to our 'old self', to take up our cross and follow after Jesus, to live by his spirit, to be guided by his teachings and the example of his life.

To be baptized, to become a Christian, is not only to receive an abundance of blessings and resources of strength, but to enter into a life of persecution and suffering. It is to place ourselves on the side of the outcast and the rejected, on the side of the 'losers' rather than the 'winners'. It is to become automatically a part of the 'moral minority' in this world. That is precisely the way Jesus conceived of his baptism. He knew that it involved hardship. He realized that it would result in taking up a cross. At first his disciples rejected this idea. They looked to the rewards rather than to the cost of discipleship. They beheld the vision of a crown bereft of a cross.

Jesus had to insist over and over again that they accept the hard realities of the Christian life. When he first told them that it would be his lot to suffer and finally be killed, Peter was adamant. "No", he said, "this shall not be." And Jesus turned on him with a startling ferocity, "Get behind me Satan". (Matt. 16:22-23) Again, when James and John asked him if they could receive the places of prominence in the coming Kingdom and be seated at his right and left hand, Jesus answered them with another question, one which leaves no doubt of how he conceived of his baptism. "Are you" he said to James and John, "able to be baptized with the baptism I am baptized with?" (Matt. 20:22)

It was only much later that James and John and all the other disciples would come to understand Jesus words. Gradually they learned that taking on the baptism of Jesus, meant turning the accepted meaning of 'greatness' upside down. Those who were least in the Kingdom, who were the servants of all, would be deemed the greatest. Those who were considered the 'losers' in the consuming quest for prestige and power and wealth would be among those who were truly the 'winners'. Those who loved a little would find more blessedness than those who owned a lot.

The truth that Jesus sought to convey to his disciples is that the life of the baptized, will never be acceptable to the powers of this world, for the way of our baptism lies in utter opposition to the way of these powers. Love for all people interferes with greed and with graft. It will not tolerate racism and prejudice. It cannot turn its back on oppression and injustice. It will not passively accept the preoccupation with preparation for war and the waging of war. In a word, it knocks the props out from under the very things upon which our world thrives and upon which it depends.

To those whose counsel is to take the easy road, Jesus still says, "Get behind me Satan". It will not do, for example, to perpetuate the popular idea that individuals are to be charitable and concerned for one another, even across racial and national boundaries, but that larger communities and nations must operate strictly on the basis of self-interest. It will not due to confine our compassion to the victims of injustice while turning a blind eye to its causes. We have been taught these lies so long and so often, not only from our military and political leaders, but sad to say, even from our pulpits and theological text books, that we believe them.

Each one of us has our own part to play on the stage of life, as we act out the meaning of our baptism. It may be a very limited role, private and personal. It may be a much wider one, social and political in its scope. But we must not shrink from the part we are given. And if we attempt to live out our baptism, as best we are able; then from time to time, for us too, the heavens will open, and we will hear in our hearts words of commendation that give us the strength to carry on the work Jesus has bequeathed to us, "to fulfill all righteousness."

2nd Sunday After the Epiphany

The Lamb and the World

John 1: 29-41

> *The next day he (John the Baptist) saw Jesus coming toward him, and said, "Behold, the Lamb of God, who takes away the sin of the world! This is he of whom I said, 'After me comes a man who ranks before me, for he was before me.' I myself did not know him; but for this I came baptizing with water, that he might be revealed to Israel." And John bore witness, I saw the Spirit descend as a dove from heaven, and it remained on him. I myself did not know him; but he who sent me to baptize with water said to me, 'He on whom you see the Spirit descend and remain, this is he who baptizes with the Holy Spirit.' And I have seen and have borne witness that this is the Son of God. The next day again John was standing with two of his disciples; and he looked at Jesus as he walked, and said, "Behold, the Lamb of God!" The two disciples heard him say this, and they followed Jesus. Jesus turned, and saw them following, and said to them, "What do you seek?" And they said to him, "Rabbi" (which means Teacher), "where are you staying?" He said to them, "Come and see." They came and saw where he was staying; and they stayed with him that day, for it was about the tenth hour. One of the two who heard John speak, and followed him, was Andrew, Simon Peter's brother. He first found his brother Simon, and said to him, "We have found the Messiah" (which means Christ).*

"Behold the Lamb of God, who takes away the sin of the world." For nearly 1300 years the Church has incorporated those words in a beautiful communion hymn known as the Agnus Dei, and sung them just before the bread and wine are distributed in the

Lord's Supper. What caused John the Baptist to speak these words when he looked up and saw Jesus approaching on that day long ago? It's almost as if he had been granted some unique intuition as to the meaning of Jesus' life.

How should we understand these words that we have repeated and sung so many times? The reference of Scripture to the Messiah under the figure of a lamb is most clearly contained in the 53rd chapter of Isaiah, verse 7, "He was oppressed and he was afflicted, yet he opened not his mouth; like a lamb that is led to the slaughter." This symbol of Jesus as the lamb of God is in keeping with the Old Testament emphasis on the importance of sacrifice as an atonement for sin. But we should note that in this same passage, Isaiah also describes the Messiah as the one who identifies with all that is human in the form of a suffering servant. The key words, well known to us through Handel's "Messiah", are contained in verses 3 through 6: "He was despised and rejected by men, a man of sorrows and acquainted with grief. ...Surely he has borne our griefs and carried our sorrows...and the Lord has laid on him the iniquity of us all."

The picture of an innocent little lamb being led away to be slaughtered, fails, however, to contain the full meaning and power of the Baptist's words. They were not spoken of one who at the time was persecuted, suffering or dying. John's words, "Behold, the Lamb of God", contain a vision of hope and of promise. It is the vision of one who comes from God and who identifies completely with us. So Jesus spoke often of all humanity as sheep, sheep who had strayed from the fold, sheep without a shepherd, sheep misled by false shepherds, in need of a Good Shepherd.

We human beings, living in a world of sin, are like lambs being led to the slaughter. We wander here and there, looking for greener pastures, often lost and lonely. We live lonely lives that seem devoid of meaning and whose certain end is death. It is this life, with its sorrows and griefs, its heavy burdens, its lack of hope, its discouragements and despair, that the Lamb of God shares with us. The vision of the Lamb is of one who in that identification with our sinful human nature, unites us with the presence and power of God. The vision of the Lamb of God is of one who brings us hope and joy and peace in the midst of this life and this world.

But John's description of Jesus as the Lamb of God was not confined to that of solidarity with our humanity. It was also that of the conquering lamb, the Victor over sin and death and despair. It was a vision of his majesty and might. "After me comes a man who ranks before me, for he was before me." It was a vision later captured in words that portrayed the Lamb as one "who sits upon the throne" and to whom is ascribed "blessing and honor and glory and might...from every creature in heaven and on earth and under the earth and in the sea and all therein." (Rev.5:13)

It is important that we catch the universal aspect of the Baptist's vision, emphasized in this passage from Revelations, "The Lamb of God who takes away the sin of the world". John's words convey the great truth that Jesus' work and mission of redemption is valid for all of humanity and for the whole earth. It was a vision later voiced by the writer of this gospel in those well-known words, "God so loved the world, that he gave his only begotten son." (John 3:16)

It is God's love that binds us all together in interdependence and interrelationship, each and every human life, and every living thing, animals, fish, plants, trees, the oceans, the mountains, the plains and the valleys, the flowers of the field and the birds of the air. Everything in all creation is purified and made infinitely precious by the redeeming power of that love made manifest in the Lamb of God who takes away the sin of the world. For as St. Paul writes in his letter to the Colossians, "in him all things were created in heaven and on earth...and in him all things hold together." (Col.1:16-17)

This oft repeated Biblical theme of a universal love which joins together and unites all things in the created world is one that shapes the way we live and act in our daily lives. It causes us to look askance upon every form of flag-waving pride which calls itself 'patriotism', but whose purpose is to turn us against other groups and designate them as enemies, rather than as fellow-human beings. It motivates us to reject every appeal to separate ourselves from those fellow human beings by reason of our skin color, or social standing, or religion. The Lamb of God we acknowledge as Lord came to take away the sin of the <u>world</u>. There is no way that we can turn our particular understanding of the Christian faith into an instrument that divides us from those who view God differently than we do. To do so is to turn our backs upon the universality of God's love. This does not mean that we close our eyes to the real differences that separate us from others on so many levels. But it does mean that we refuse to let these differences divide us and blind us to our fundamental unity, our common humanity and value as the children of the creator God. That overarching truth serves as the basic chart and compass of our life.

And what is true about our relationship to other human beings is also true about our kinship with all of life and with the earth itself. The wholistic view of all life as intimately interrelated, expressed so beautifully in the religions of Native American Indians, is clearly implied in the Christian revelation that God's redemptive action includes the whole world. If any part of this world is diminished, each of us is reduced to that same extent. If any species of life is threatened or extinguished through our rapaciousness, or if any part of our earth is ravaged and abused because of our selfishness and greed, we eventually suffer too, for we are tied to the earth as we are to its Creator. To despise one is to despise the other, and to love one is to love both. If we believe this, then we will treat the earth from which we have come and to which we return, with gentleness and gratitude and respect.

The magnificent vision of the John the Baptist, who was somehow enabled to see in Jesus, "the Lamb of God who takes away the sin of the world," tells us a great deal about who we are and what our place is in the whole scheme of things. At the same time it provides us with a direction and purpose in our daily lives. Just as Jesus later called the disciples of John to come and see where he lived, to follow him, to live as he lived, to do his work, so he calls us to love and care for the earth, to use our life and expend it on behalf of others, to be with Him, a lamb of God, contributing our own small part, in helping to take away the sin of the world.

God's Kingdom Here and Now

Matthew 4: 12-23

> *Now when he (Jesus) heard that John (the Baptist) had been arrested he withdrew into Galilee; and leaving Nazareth he went and dwelt in Capernaum by the sea, in the territory of Zebulun and Naphtali, that what was spoken by the prophet Isaiah might be fulfilled: "The land of Zebulun and the land of Naphtali, toward the sea, across the Jordan, Galilee of the Gentiles-the people who sat in darkness have seen a great light, and for those who sat in the region and shadow of death light has dawned." From that time Jesus began to preach, saying, "Repent, for the kingdom of heaven is at hand." As he walked by the Sea of Galilee, he saw two brothers, Simon, who is called Peter and Andrew his brother, casting a net into the sea; for they were fishermen. And he said to them, "Follow me, and I will make you fishers of men." Immediately they left their nets and followed him. And going on from there he saw two other brothers, James the son of Zebedee and John his brother, in the boat with Zebedee their father, mending their nets, and he called them. Immediately they left the boat and their father, and followed him. And he went about Galilee teaching in their synagogues and preaching the gospel of the kingdom and healing every disease and every infirmity among the people.*

Like his forerunner, John the Baptist, the basic theme of Jesus teaching and preaching dealt with the Kingdom of God. This theme is twice reiterated in the text from the 4th Chapter of Matthew. In verse 17 we read, "From that time Jesus began to preach, saying, "Repent, for the Kingdom of heaven is at hand"; and in verse 23 we are told that "he went about all Galilee teaching in their synagogues and preaching the gospel of the kingdom..."

It is important to understand that the terms "kingdom of heaven" and "kingdom of God" mean exactly the same thing and are used interchangeably in the Scriptures. They refer to the benevolent, wise, and just rule of God. It is a place where oppression, poverty, hunger, disease and death itself have been vanquished, where people live in peace and harmony with one another and with their environment.

In the real world, this concept of the kingdom of God appears to be outside the realm of possibility. It seems entirely Utopian, a wishful dream. As a result, it has most often been understood only in some futuristic sense. It is confined to some other world, to a life beyond this one, to heaven.

But Jesus words on this subject convey something quite different. Jesus said "the kingdom of heaven is at hand." By that he meant it is breaking into the present, into this world and this life. He often pointed to himself as the manifestation of that kingdom on earth. So he went about doing good, and as our text says "healing every disease and every infirmity among the people". Jesus referred to such acts of healing as a clear sign of God's kingdom. Once after loosening the tongue of a person who was dumb he said, "If I by the finger of God cast out demons, then the kingdom of God has come upon you."(Luke 11:20)

Jesus also taught quite explicitly that we do not need to hunt and search for the kingdom or look for it to come in some future life. When the Pharisees asked him when the kingdom of God was coming, he replied that it would not appear with "signs to be observed; nor will they say, "Lo here it is! or there! for behold, the kingdom of God is in the midst of you."(Luke 17:21) His advice was in effect, "Don't keep looking for God's Kingdom in some other place or some other time, it is right here, right now. It is in your midst. It is being unfolded before your very eyes. While you gaze up into the sky looking for some cosmic event, some transcendental vision, the kingdom is taking shape at your feet. Stop looking up and start looking down and around you, into the faces of your fellow human beings and onto the earth where your feet are squarely planted, where the presence and power of God's kingdom are unfolding before your very eyes.

In the 13th Chapter of Matthew Jesus teaches us further about the earthly nature of God's kingdom through the use of parables. He compares the kingdom of heaven to tiny seeds which are planted into the ground, some of which grow and produce fruit.(v. 1-9) Even the smallest seed of all may shoot up into a shrub or tree large enough to provide a shelter and nesting place for the birds.(v. 31-32) Again he compares it to a treasure hidden in a field, which when uncovered brought great joy to its finder.(v.44) It is significant that the focus for the presence and growth of the kingdom in nearly all of these parables is the ground or the earth.

"The kingdom of heaven is at hand." The splendor and glory of the Kingdom of heaven shines out in this humble here and now. Just as the precious gift of the Incarnation was conveyed in the humble surrounding of a manger and the lowly shepherds and their sheep, so with the kingdom he came to inaugurate. Like Jesus himself, the kingdom brings light to the world, as Isaiah foretold, "to the people who walk in darkness ...to those who dwell in a land of deep darkness".(Is.9:2) It results not only in the healing of diseases of every kind, physical, mental, and spiritual,(Matt.4:23), but in the realization of a more just society, as Isaiah again envisions, "The yoke of his burden, and the staff for his shoulder, the rod of his oppressor, thou hast broken."(Is.9:4)

Jesus came preaching "the gospel of the kingdom". The very word kingdom comes from the realm of the political. It refers not only to an inner chamber within the human heart and mind, but to people in community, to societies and nations and to the world as a whole. And yet somehow we have tried to confine this teaching of the kingdom, if not just to a future life, then to a completely personal and private sphere. When we say that a minister should stick "to preaching the gospel" we really mean that one should not relate the gospel to politics or to worldly affairs. Yet, Jesus preached a "gospel of the kingdom" and the 'good news' of the kingdom he preached was the proclamation of God's Lordship over all the world and everything in it. The kingdom of God stands in judgment over all forms of human societies and communities. It condemns the injustice of capitalism and communism and socialism and every other ideology upon the face of the earth. It denounces them precisely to the extent that they fail to realize justice and equal opportunity and freedom and full access for all people to the necessities of life, such as food and clothing and shelter and medical care.

It is indeed true that this kingdom Jesus came to inaugurate, carries within it the vision and hope of a perfect society, of a community where the power of sin and evil are overthrown and defeated. And our human response to this is that the kingdom of God is Utopian, an impossible dream that raises our hopes only to cruelly crush them against the hard rocks of reality. We will always have the poor with us, there will always be wars and rumors of war. Aren't these words right in the Bible? Crime and class conflict and racial intolerance and injustices of every kind are as eradicable from human society as the seven deadly sins are from human nature.

So what is the answer? The answer must be that God sent Jesus as the personification of a perfect divine kingdom right into the midst of this evil world. And the result was that this world is redeemed and made better and shares in the perfection whose fullness belongs to God alone. To view the kingdom of God as something which is only to be anticipated in another world or in another life is to look with distain upon the faith that God brought that kingdom into the midst of our present life. To contend that the kingdom of God is either only an impossible dream or a purely future ideal is at heart the manifestation of a lack of faith. It is an act of unbelief.

The fact that God's kingdom cannot be fully realized in this world, in no wise relegates its purpose to some other world or some other time. The kingdom of God is a guide which points like a compass in the darkness of night and the turmoil of storm in the direction of God's will. It points in the direction of those civil laws and political realities which can actually lift up the down trodden and give hope to the oppressed. The kingdom of God is a power which energizes us to stand up for what we know is right and fair, even when it means flying in the face of the majority opinion, even when it means that, like Jesus, we will face opposition and persecution. The kingdom of God is a present hope that keeps us striving and working to realize a better world and a more just society, in the face of discouragement and disheartenment and seeming failure.

This teaching and this hope is summed up in the familiar words that Jesus taught us to pray, "Your kingdom come, on earth, as it is in heaven."... You and I are not only called to pray that prayer, but to work for its fulfillment.

4th Sunday After the Epiphany

True Happiness

Matthew 5:1-12

> *Seeing the crowds, he went up on the moun-tain, and when he sat down his disciples came to him. And he opened his mouth and taught them, saying: "Blessed are the poor in spirit, for theirs is the king-dom of heaven. Blessed are those who mourn, for they shall be comforted. Blessed are the meek, for they shall inherit the earth. Blessed are those who hunger and thirst for righteousness, for they shall be satisfied. Blessed are the merciful, for they shall obtain mercy. Blessed are the pure in heart, for they shall see God. Blessed are the peacemakers, for they shall be called sons of God. Blessed are those who are persecuted for righteousness' sake, for theirs is the kingdom of heaven. Blessed are you when men revile you and persecute you and utter all kinds of evil against you falsely on my account. Rejoice and be glad, for your reward is great in heaven, for so men persecuted the prophets who were before you."*

The passage of Scripture in which Matthew's gospel in-troduces the main body of Jesus teachings, is known to us as the Beatitudes. These opening words to what we call the Sermon on the Mount are in effect Jesus' depiction of the life-style of his dis-ciples. He describes his followers as those who find blessedness, true happiness, as a result of certain convictions and concerns which characterize their lives.

Jesus words raise the question of how one finds happiness in this life. Is it a matter of good luck? Does it come from having enough and more than enough material possessions? Does it con-sist of good health and relative freedom from problems or troubles and sorrows? Who could deny that any or all of these things add to the enjoyment of life? Yet the blessedness which Jesus describes makes no reference to them at all. It ignores them completely. It turns upside down the popular T.V. concepts of happiness with which we are daily indoctrinated. It has nothing in common with the voices which keep drumming into our minds that happiness is owning a big car or a big home, that it is a high-paying job, or winning the lottery; that it is a beautiful body, or expensive clothes, or a fashionable hair-do; that it is a life of leisure, vacations in the sun, travel to lands of intrigue, or that it is being envied, admired and praised.

It is because our search for happiness is conducted with such earnestness, almost desperation, that it has become big business, a primary theme that advertisers hold out to us for a price. "We can give you happiness. Just listen to us. Buy our products, follow our directions. Purchase these kits. Enter these contests"... and the voices go on, and people listen!

Listen instead to what Jesus tells us in this text! He says that real happiness consists in things totally different from these popular prescriptions. Real happiness consists not so much in what we possess as in what we are able to give. It arises not so much in freedom from pain and problems as in the ability to share the hurts of life with others. It is realized not so much in being liked and admired, as in the doing of what is good and right and just. Happiness results from becoming pure in heart, meek, and poor in spirit. Happiness consists in being aware of our human limitations and needs. It lies in knowing that we cannot do everything, be everything, accomplish everything. It is the result of recognizing our dependence upon God and our fellow human beings, of realizing that we cannot go it alone. It comes from being open to God's help which is always near and available. It is the opposite of that proud spirit which insists that we alone are the captain of our ship and masters of our fate. According to Jesus, happiness lies in the desire to learn more, to serve more, to love more. It is hungering and thirsting for righteousness. It is being merciful. It is making peace. This is drastically different from the prevalent idea that happiness consists in satisfying the drive to have more or to possess more.

We often attempt to motivate young people to take their education seriously, to attend classes regularly and to study harder, by assuring them that doing these things will eventually enable them to make more money and obtain a higher standard of living. What is promised may or may not be true. But what is implied is that these things will also make for greater happiness in their lives, and that is not necessarily true at all. Unless learning itself becomes a joy, unless the knowledge and the skills acquired are directed in some way toward serving their fellow human beings,unless our children learn not only to be mercenary, but merciful, not only to make money but to make peace, not only to hunger for riches but for righteousness, then the fire which drives them toward materialistic reward, may turn to ashes once it has been acquired.

Jesus is right when he insists that in the final analysis, true happiness simply cannot be defined in materialistic terms. Therein lies the fallacy of those in the Western industrialized world who hold up before others the golden face of capitalism as a kind of god which can insure a higher standard of living, better cars, and superior technology. This may be true at least for the short haul, although the reasons for it are not always so palatable as we like to think. Behind the smiling mask of a higher living standard for some, hides the grim face of greed and poverty for many. A decent standard of living and access to the basic necessities of life for all people in every society is a goal worth pursuing. The desire to realize it is in essence a desire for righteousness, and for justice. Jesus is telling us that true happiness is not realized so much in the personal possession of this basic human right as in the passion to attain it, not only for myself, but for others. In a word, Jesus directs our pursuit of happiness along that pathway of action prescribed by the prophet Micah; in doing justice, in loving kindness, and in walking humbly with our God.(Micah 6:8)

Jesus describes another path to happiness that sounds not only strange but absurd. He says that it is discovered in the process of being persecuted for the sake of righteousness, that it is found in the midst of grief or affliction. It would, indeed, be a perverted and warped kind of bliss that would actually seek out sorrow, suffering or persecution in order to feel good. Psychology has rightly described this concept of happiness as an aberration called masochism. But the happiness Jesus here describes is a far cry from pursuing pain in order to experience pleasure. Jesus is merely pointing here to a rugged reality of life in this world. There is no lasting escape from trouble and sorrow. Drugs offer only temporary relief at best, and in the end, deeper despair. Certainly there is no evasion of sickness and death. But in the midst of pain and of tears, God's comfort comes in the understanding and love that we show one another. This comfort, which the compassionate convey to each other, is not a kind of happiness that one actively seeks to experience. But to give or receive it in the time of need, is to realize a kind of joy and blessedness on the part of both giver and receiver that is uniquely uplifting. It is what St. Paul referred to when he wrote to the Corinthians, "Blessed be the God and Father of our Lord Jesus Christ...who comforts us in all our affliction, so that we may be able to comfort those who are in any affliction, with the comfort with which we ourselves are comforted by God".(2 Cor.1:3-4)

Finally, Jesus says that happiness is not only discovered in the midst of life's unavoidable sorrows, but arises in the midst of suffering persecution and rejection for the things we believe and do. This happiness in no way eliminates the physical pain nor the hurt of rejection and loneliness that accompanies persecution. Rather it is a joy that goes beyond pain, that penetrates more deeply than any hurt. It is a happiness that cannot be taken away, that nothing can destroy. It is a happiness that endures. It is a happiness that arises from knowing that you have done what you know in your heart is right, from having refused to disown what you most deeply believe, from having stood up for what you were convinced was the will of God, and therefore what was best for your fellow human beings. That is an action whose reward may be enhanced in heaven, but it does not wait for heaven. It is experienced in the present. As Jesus says "Blessed are those who are persecuted for righteousness sake for theirs is the Kingdom of Heaven." It is theirs here and now.

The happiness of the believer, does not ultimately depend on what we usually consider good luck or good fortune, nor does it spring from the sources to which we are so persistently directed. It is rather based upon our openness to Love and our willingness to share that Love, even in the face of difficulty and opposition. This kind of happiness is one of the chief characteristic of those who follow Christ. It is written on their faces. It is inscribed indelibly upon their lives. It is visible in their actions. Like the believers that Jesus describes in the parable of the Last Judgment, they may not be aware that the happiness they experience is a profound witness to others of their faith, but it is.

A cartoon I once saw showed ushers dumping large baskets filled to the brim with offerings on the the desk of the minister, while he rummages wildly through his sermon notes, mumbling over and over, "What did I say?". Although the sermon has its importance, the most effective and powerful witness to faith may not be found in the sermonizing at all. It is transmitted not so much in what we say, as in what we are and in what we do. It is to be found in our body language, our smile, our endurance in trouble, our patience in suffering, our pursuit of righteousness and justice. It is to be found in that happiness which glows like a halo around the believer, and which radiates out in the deeds that make a difference.

5th Sunday After the Epiphany

Salt and Light

Matthew 5:13-20

> *"You are the salt of the earth; but if salt has lost its taste, how shall its saltness be restored? It is no longer good for anything except to be thrown out and trodden under foot by men." "You are the light of the world. A city set on hill cannot be hid. Nor do men light a lamp and put it under a bushel, but on a stand, and it gives light to all in the house. Let your light so shine before men, that they may see your good works and give glory to your Father who is in heaven." "Think not that I have come to abolish the law and the prophets; I have come not to abolish them but to fulfill them. For truly, I say to you, till heaven and earth pass away, not an iota, not a dot, will pass from the law until all is accomplished. Whoever then relaxes one of the least of these commandments and teaches men so, shall be called least in the kingdom of heaven; but he who does them and teaches them shall be called great in the kingdom of heaven. For I tell you, unless your righteousness exceeds that of the scribes and Pharisees, you will never enter the kingdom of heaven."*

In his "Sermon on the Mount" Jesus describes the life which is directed by faith in God. In this text he portrays the believer as the "salt of the earth", and the "light of the world".

The two primary purposes of salt are to preserve food from spoiling and to give it flavor. Of these, the first function is the most important. In Jesus day, 'before refrigeration' it was absolutely essential. "You are the salt of the earth" means that the life of a believer fulfills the indispensable function of helping to preserve the entire earth and all living things from corruption and decay. This is done by simply giving expression to the faith that is in us. Still it is possible for this faith to remain dormant, to take on no tangible embodiment in terms of actual deeds of love. It is possible that in the face of a moral and political corruption and rottenness which stinks in the nostrils of God, we who have the capacity to act as salt, simply stand and stare and find excuses for our failure to be what we are. When this happens then we have become like salt whose saltiness has been diluted or destroyed. Then we may be good in our hearts, but we are still good for nothing. When, as believers, we no longer fulfill the function of salt, preserving the earth from corruption, then it is also true, that we no longer add zest and flavor and meaning, either to our own existence or to that of those around us. Just as salt that has lost its saltiness is really no longer salt at all, so is a faith which fails to act in love, no longer faith at all. It may still have the name but its essence is gone.

Jesus also said, "You are the light of the world." Notice that the witness of the believer's faith is universal in scope. It is the salt of the <u>earth</u>. It is the light of the <u>world</u>. We are not the salt and light of the Church, or even of the nation, but of the earth, which God loves and cares for in its entirety and without distinction or restriction or respect of persons.

The purpose of light in the moral sense in which Jesus uses it here, is to dispel the darkness of ignorance, and injustice and evil and oppression. We who have been blessed with light, who have become 'enlightened' by faith, are to let our light shine into the dark corners where evil and wickedness prevails. That does not mean our own little light will illuminate the whole world, but that it can cast its glow upon some small area of it, and in particular the place where we live and work and worship. I recall a song we used to sing with much fervor when I was a child in a small-town Nebraska Sunday School, "Brighten the corner where you are". That's the task which Jesus designated as our own when he said, "You are the light of the world".

But again, it is possible to have light in ourselves, to have received the gift of faith, and still hide it, or even extinguish it. It is possible that instead of allowing our light to shine, instead of putting our lamp of faith on a stand so that it sheds light on all around us, that we put it under a bushel, where no one can see it or benefit from it.

Let your light shine, Jesus says. Don't hide it, don't cover it up. Don't be ashamed of it. As another children's hymn puts it, "This little light of mine, let it shine, all the time, let it shine." Jesus wouldn't urge us to do what appears so obvious, if the temptation to hide our light, to cover it up, wasn't a real one.

It is in fact easy to give in to the temptation to dim or extinguish the light of faith in the face of evil's scary challenges. How simple to manufacture plausible and even high-sounding excuses for hiding our light. How effortless to drop the light, drift with the current and move with the crowd. We can look around at our world and in our own community and see clearly the evidences of oppression and injustice and prejudice and moral corruption. We behold a system of taxation that literally robs the poor of the little they need for the necessities of life, that diverts huge sums to build weapons of war while large numbers of our citizens have no health insurance or medical coverage and no means of obtaining it. We behold these and a myriad of other evils that we know are an offense to the God in whom we believe, and whose light we share. But there is great pressure to hide the light, and seemingly plausible reasons for doing so. After all we must be prudent, and patient and understanding. Give things time to change. Those who perpetrate these evils and give assent to them are good people. We must show them first that we are their friends, then in the future we may be allowed to witness to the truth, to speak up for justice. It is poor strategy to pursue a policy of confrontation, to rupture possible gains by being prematurely outspoken. Go along with things, don't turn anyone off, bide your time, and the moment will arrive when the light can prudently be slipped out from under the bushel.

There is a modicum of truth in this advice, enough to make it doubly dangerous. For the most part it is devoid of Scriptural authority, or much practical success. The fact of the matter is that the real reason we are most often tempted to hide our light is fear. It is the fear of unpleasant consequences, the fear of losing our friends, our popularity, even our jobs. These are basic fears and they strike hard and deep . They are fears capable of making cowards of us all.

Most of us are ready and willing to let the light of our faith shine if it brings us honor and good will. But, its most likely result is the exact opposite. Let the light shine into dark places, scatter salt on the open sores of evil, and the result is often disrepute, ill will and even persecution. And Jesus said, consider this a blessing, and discover real happiness in the act of serving God within the fellowship of the faithful.

Finally, reflect upon the fact that the purpose of both salt and light are active and utilitarian. They cannot speak. Words are not their business. Their function is practical. They do something constructive in the real world in which we live. They halt corruption and expose evil. They preserve the right and illuminate the good. In a word, they do needful things. They do not preach good words. They perform good works. They are not plausible words of wisdom but a demonstration of power. Where did we ever get the idea that faith and good works somehow exist in division from each other, that faith is the result of grace, and good works are a kind of legalism whereby we try to win God's love? Legalism may describe how "good works" can be perverted, just as faith itself can be misused. The letter of James has it right, "Faith by itself, if it has no works, is dead." and "I by my works will show you my faith."(James 2:17-18) St. Paul basically agreed when he described faith as "working through love."(Gal.5:6)

Jesus never attempted to tear apart the seamless robe of faith and good works. That is why he insisted that he did not "come to abolish the law and the prophets", but to "fulfill them". The true teaching of Judaism found in the Old Testament is that the one who believes in God loves the Law of God, and seeks with heart and mind and soul to do it. It was a perversion of that Law by the scribes and Pharisees which St. Paul condemned as opposed to the way of faith. Yet St. Paul also insisted that the Law properly understood was "holy and just and good".(Romans 7:12)

The Christian life and witness, like that of Jesus himself, is not opposed to anything in the law or the prophets. It opposes only their perversion. That is why Jesus says that our righteousness must exceed that of the scribes and the Pharisees. Jesus will not tolerate any interpretation of the Law that lifts the ritual of worship, above the ethical task of justice, which places traditions or culturally derived codes of conduct above the great commandment of God to love our neighbor as ourself. It is this Law of love which constitutes the heart of the teachings of Moses and the prophets and Jesus. It is a love which flows freely from faith, like water from an artesian well. It is a love which is salt to the earth and light to the world.

6th Sunday After the Epiphany

Inside Out

Matt. 5:20-37

> "For I tell you, unless your righteousness exceeds that of the scribes and Pharisees, you will never enter the kingdom of heaven. You have heard that it was said to the men of old, 'You shall not kill; and whoever kills shall be liable to judgment.' But I say to you that everyone who is angry with his brother shall be liable to judgment; whoever insults his brother shall be liable to the council, and whoever says, 'You fool!' shall be liable to the hell of fire. So if you are offering your gift at the altar, and there remember that your brother has something against you, leave your gift there before the altar and go; first be reconciled to your brother, and then come and offer your gift. Make friends quickly with your accuser, while you are going with him to court, lest your accuser hand you over to the judge, and the judge to the guard, and you be put in prison; truly, I say to you, you will never get out till you have paid the last penny. You have heard that it was said, 'You shall not commit adultery.' But I say to you that every one who looks at a woman lustfully has already committed adultery with her in his heart. If your right eye causes you to sin, pluck it out and throw it away; it is better that you lose one of your members than that your whole body be thrown into hell. And if your right hand causes you to sin, cut it off and throw it away; it is better that you lose one of your members than that your whole body go into hell. It was also said, 'Whoever divorces his wife, let him give her a certificate of divorce.' But I say to you that unchastity, makes her an adulteress; and whoever marries a divorced woman commits adultery.

It is important to keep in mind that the Bible is both an inspired and at the same time a human book. St. Paul wrote, we "have this treasure in earthen vessels."(2 Cor. 4:7)

This is borne out by the story of how the Scriptures came into being. For several years following his death the stories about Jesus were passed on by word of mouth and only later written down. Then several different accounts were recorded, and from these various records, the writers of the Gospels compiled their narratives. Most scholars believe that Mark's chronicle was the earliest, and that both Matthew and Luke incorporated large parts of Mark into their own. In addition they both had access to several other sources. It is understandable that the individual writers had certain points of view or interpretations of Jesus ministry and teaching which they wished to emphasize and this to a certain extent determined in what order and to what specific purpose they joined together the common core of material contained in the accounts available to them.

It is evident that the writer of Matthew's gospel wants to show how Jesus was the fulfillment of the Old Testament prophecy and of the Law. Jesus is seen as the bringer of a new Law which goes beyond that of the Old Testament. This concept of a 'new' Law became the source of much debate within the early Church, which from its nativity was plagued with division.(ICor. I:10-17) One source of dissension among early Christians regarded the matter of divorce.

Jesus teaching on the subject, both in this text and in Matthew 19, as well as in Mark and Luke, appears from our modern view, rigid to the point of being deficient in human compassion. Yet when viewed from the practice of the time, Jesus opposed a widely prevalent and well established custom, which allowed a husband to divorce his wife almost at will. In his day a woman had little or no protection and was treated like an item of property. In this sense Jesus prohibition against nearly all divorce can be seen as a protection of the rights of the woman.

The most disconcerting part of this Scripture, however, is the passage contained in verses 21-22 and 27-28, where Matthew quotes Jesus as saying that in effect, murder and anger on the one hand and adultery and lust on the other, are equally malicious and deserving of a similar judgment or punishment. Here it would appear that Matthew's concern to compare the Old Testament Law to a 'higher law', advocated by Jesus, was so strong that it led to a certain distortion of Jesus' real teaching. I do not make this assertion lightly, nor without considerable hesitation. But a number of things lead me to this conclusion.

First, there is no parallel to these particular precepts in any of the other Gospels, nor in the entire Bible. Secondly, they do not harmonize with the whole body of Jesus teachings. It appears that the primary intent of the writer in this passage is one which is quoted in Matthew 15:11 and is contained also in Mark 7:21. ("what comes out of a man is what defiles a man") It is the simple but profound insight that the inner thoughts exercise a potent influence upon outward actions.

Thoughts are important. They lead toward corresponding acts. That is why St. Paul counsels the Philippians, "Whatever is true,...honorable, ...just...pure...lovely...gracious...think about these things". (Phil. 4:8) Good advice? Positive thinking! But we are human. Our thoughts cannot always be positive. Sometimes we get angry, and it is understandable that we do. There is much that happens in this life to get angry about. So St. Paul writes, "Be angry, but do not sin", and he adds, "do not let the sun go down on your anger".(Eph.4:26) Again this is sound advice, particularly if you want to get a good night's sleep. Yet anger is an emotion that can be utilized for good as well as evil. There is a righteous anger, an anger directed against injustice and evil of all kinds, that was clearly expressed by the Old Testament prophets and by Jesus himself. We need to get angry at the right things and express our anger in a constructive manner. The same sort of thing can be said about lust. Sexual desire can result in the most wonderful expressions of love known to human beings. Its energies may be redirected in other creative channels such as art or literature or work of various kinds and service to our fellow human beings.

Because our thoughts have such great significance it is important that we try to keep in touch with them, to be aware as much as possible of what we are really feeling deep down inside.

There are a number of things that can aid us in this endeavor. We need to take time to be quiet, to meditate, to examine our thoughts, to analyze and understand them. Looking at our dreams can help us to get at some of the feelings that tend to lurk undercover and hide from our conscious scrutiny. The more alert we can be to our inner feelings the more able we are to express them and direct them into constructive channels.

It is the unexpressed desires or angers, about which we feel so much guilt or fear that we repress them and deny their existence, which represent a clear and present danger. That is why Jesus so urgently reminds us that it is from within, out of the heart, that destructive actions may erupt.

But how can we explain Jesus words in verses 29 and 30 of our text, where following his comment on lust and adultery, he says that if our eye or hand or foot causes us to sin it is better to pluck out or cut off the offending parts than to let the whole body be destroyed. Once again it would appear that the writer of Matthew has taken words that Jesus originally spoke in a different context and applied them here for the purposes referred to above.

These same words appear in Mark (9:42-48) and are again quoted by Matthew (18:6-9) in connection with Jesus' condemnation of those who cause "one of these little ones" to sin. First Jesus says that it would be better for such a one that a "great millstone were hung round his neck and he was thrown into the sea". Then come the words about cutting off the hand or foot, or plucking out the eye if they are the causes of this offence. Both of these statements are obviously exaggerations. Jesus had no intention that they be taken literally. But they express his abhorrence at the act of causing one of "these little ones" to stumble. The extremity of language he uses in condemning it points to the terrible seriousness of the sin. And who are "the little ones"? They are the 'little people', the powerless, the downtrodden, the poor, the insignificant and the overlooked. There is no greater sin against our Maker, so far as Jesus is concerned, than to treat people with contempt and disdain. Contempt for a fellow human being, created like ourselves in the image of God, is the most deadly of all transgressions. It not only destroys another human being but oneself as well.

The words of Jesus which Matthew records in our text are a commentary on this truth. "Whoever is angry with his brother shall be liable to judgment; whoever <u>insults</u> his brother shall be liable to the council, and whoever says '<u>you Fool</u>', shall be liable to the hell of fire." Here Jesus makes it clear that contempt, scorn, and disdain are among the supreme offenses against the humanity which God created and loves. It is better to be angry at someone than to think nothing of them or to believe that they are unworthy of any consideration.

Finally, we must add that Jesus insight about the importance of one's thoughts in regard to how one acts has tremendous social and political ramifications. We live in a day where the consumption of drugs, and violent crime cause widespread concern and fear. The very foundations of our society are sorely threatened. Many people believe that the answer lies in stricter law enforcement, more severe punishment, bigger jails, the death penalty. The teaching of Jesus makes it clear that any real solution to our problems must <u>exceed</u> these proposals. We must be concerned about the causes of increasing drug consumption, the causes of violence and crime. We must be willing to look at the despair and loss of hope and the resulting anger and rage which lead to these actions. This is not to say that violence can go unrestrained or crime unpunished. But law enforcement and jails are not enough. Far from it. The Law can only judge and punish the outward act. But justice and love can cure the 'inside' causes of violence.

Jesus was right when he spoke of contempt for one of these little ones as the great offense. He condemns the contempt which lacks concern for the real and agonizing needs of people such as food, clothing, decent housing, jobs and health care. He condemns the contempt which contends that other things, like jails or military arsenals, are more important than human justice.

This contempt may be the greatest single cause of violence and crime in our nation today. Jesus calls us to look within our hearts and the hearts of others, and to see that what we need most is not more judgment but more justice; not more law, but more love. The fate of our community and our world hangs in the balance. The Love Jesus came to reveal can lead us out of contempt to concern. It can lead us to be reconciled with our brothers and sisters, who need us and we them, and to do it now.

7th Sunday After the Epiphany

Love Your Enemies? Be Perfect?

Matthew 5:38-48

> Jesus taught them, saying, "You have heard that it was said, 'An eye for an eye and a tooth for a tooth.' But I say to you, Do not resist one who is evil. But if any one strikes you on the right cheek, turn to him the other also; and if any one would sue you and take your coat, let him have your cloak as well; and if any one forces you to go one mile, go with him two miles. Give to him who begs from you, and do not refuse him who would borrow from you. You have heard that it was said, 'You shall love your neighbor and hate your enemy.' But I say to you, Love your enemies and pray for those who persecute you, so that you may be sons of your Father who is in heaven; for he makes his sun rise on the evil and on the good, and sends rain on the just and on the unjust. For if you love those who love you, what reward have you? Do not even the tax collectors do the same? And if you salute only your brethren, what more are you doing than others? Do not even the Gentiles do the same? You, therefore, must be perfect, as your heavenly Father is perfect."

The teachings of Jesus contained in this portion of the Sermon on the Mount are invariably received with a curious mixture of admiration and skepticism. We admire them because they articulate such high and holy ideals, non-violence, generosity, and altruism. But on the other hand we have our doubts as to whether they are really applicable to our human situation. They seem so implausible, impractical, and unattainable. They appear to hold before us an impossible ideal. How can we remain passive in the face of evil, turn the other cheek, give more than we are asked or required, love our enemies? And how in the world can we even think of attaining perfection?

Consequently these teachings are most often interpreted as either largely or totally inaccessible to human achievement. One explanation maintains that they were intended only for a highly select group of persons willing to remain divorced from the world and devoted to a life of meditation and prayer. Another theory proposes that the utter impossibility of practicing these precepts is designed to impress us with how sinful and corrupt we really are, and in this way act as an incentive which drives us to seek God's forgiveness and the grace revealed in Christ.

But these explanations are difficult to defend. If Jesus intended that his admonitions apply only to a certain few, why didn't he say so? If, on the other hand, his words only portray an 'impossible ideal' which crushes us beneath its demand and prepares us as sinners to receive the grace of God, then we also have to accept the fact that Jesus engaged here in the questionable practice of duplicity. At the very least we have to admit that he was far from straightforward.

It seems inconceivable that Jesus would describe in such precise terms the actions which were to characterize the life of his followers, knowing that they were impossible of realization and irrelevant to our earthly existence. We must assume then that Jesus meant what he said and that his words apply to all believers. They were neither intended for the angels in heaven nor a select few, but for all of us earthlings, plain people like you and me.

This brings us back full circle to the original problem of the 'impossible ideal'. First we must understand that Jesus never meant his words to be taken in a wooden, inflexible or legalistic way. Take for example the phrase (v. 39) "Do not resist one who is evil. But if anyone strikes you on the right cheek, turn to him the other also." If taken literally and applied rigidly to every situation these words forbid believers to ever act against evil, or to behave aggressively, even in defense, against those who would injure or mistreat them or their fellow human beings. But this interpretation does not coincide with Jesus' own example. He took a vigorous and active stand against evil. He spoke harshly and even provocatively against the hypocrisy and sham of the religious leaders of his day, who placed the traditions of men above the commandments of God.(Matt.15:6) Once, when he saw people defiling God's house of prayer with commercial activities, he turned over the tables of the money changers, and physically attacked them, driving them out of the Temple courts.(Matt. 21:12-13) Furthermore, Jesus did not react in the same way on every occasion. He did not always simply 'turn the other cheek'. He chastised those who arrested him in the Garden of Gethsemane (Luke 22:52-53). When brought for questioning before the high priest and struck without cause by one of the soldiers, Jesus issued a sharp rebuke.(John 18:23)

We misunderstand these teachings about non-resistance if we look upon them as mechanical rules that fit every possible situation. Jesus taught that love is the believers most basic response, but love is not and can never be, mechanical in its operation. The counsel to 'turn the other cheek' does not mean that we are directed to accept inhumane or unjust treatment without defending our human dignity. This becomes even more true when the rights of others around us are involved. In certain situations where the welfare of a whole community is concerned it may be necessary, when all other means fail, to use physical force to defend against violent oppression and the deprivation of basic human rights. A case in point was the struggle against apartheid in South Africa.

The admonition to 'turn the other cheek' is above all not an invitation to seek physical abuse. What Jesus apparently referred to specifically was an act of deliberate insult, intended as a challenge to fight. In this ritual, a slap that was administered with the back of the right hand to the right cheek, often followed up with a harder slap with the palm to the left cheek. Jesus teaches here that we are not to fall into the trap of returning slap for slap, insult for insult, hatred for hatred, revenge for revenge. This leads only to a vicious and escalating violence, whether on a personal or communal level. To do that is to renounce the way of love and in effect to become evil's victim rather than its victor.

St. Paul summed up this truth when he wrote to the Romans "Be not overcome by evil, but overcome evil with good." (Rom. 12:21) Here we are brought back to Jesus' call to love our enemies. St. Paul, quoting Proverbs, writes, "If your enemy is hungry feed him; if he is thirsty give him drink", for by so doing you will heap burning coals upon his head." But even this advice can simply remain a way to 'punish' one's enemies by creating a 'burning shame' within them for their wrong-doings. The story is told of a missionary trying to convert a person to Christianity by quoting this passage from St. Paul. When the missionary spoke of giving food and drink to one's enemy, the 'potential convert' seemed taken aback. But when the clergyman added, "by so doing you will heap coals of fire on his head," the man fell on his knees and began to pray for his foe. When the prayer continued on and on, the priest tried to interrupt, but the man replied, "Oh no, father. Let me pray! I want to burn him right down to the stump!"

When people protest that it is impossible to love your enemies, in one sense of the word they are right. If we stick with the commonly accepted meaning of the word, 'enemy', it does involve a direct contradiction in terms. According to the dictionary your enemy is one whom you hate, toward whom you are hostile and to whom you want to do injury. It is only when we are willing to follow Jesus advice to pray for those who seek to do us harm, to look upon them as fellow human beings, to understand their faults, that the sting of bitterness and hate is removed from our hearts. Those we pray for may still look upon us as <u>their</u> enemy, but they have ceased to be <u>ours</u>. They have become instead the objects of our understanding and concern. This love is not sentimental affection. It does not even mean we agree with the other person. It is rather a kind of determined and invincible good will. So in a real sense it is right to say that in the moment we love our enemies we also cease to do so, for love has transformed them from enemies into fellow human beings.

The final words of this text are the most difficult of all, "You therefore must be perfect, as your heavenly Father is perfect". A great part of the problem here lies in the common usage of the word 'perfect' as meaning faultless or without error. That is actually a secondary meaning. The Greek word translated into English as 'perfect' is "telios" which means "the goal, or final end or completion of something". That is very similar to the primary English definition of 'perfect,' which is: "having all the essential elements and characteristics of a thing when completed, or becoming complete." The call to be perfect as God is perfect does not involve a perfection of degree but of kind. Being 'like God' is not being identical with God. It is not unusual to use this figure of speech. For instance Jesus said, "Unless you become <u>as</u> little children you cannot enter the Kingdom of God. He obviously did not mean that we must literally become a small child again, to somehow shrink in size and age. He meant that in some particular respects such as openness and trust, we become <u>like</u> little children.

So with this phrase, "you must be perfect as your Heavenly Father is perfect". It means we are to move and grow toward the goal and purpose for which we were created, i.e. to be like God. We do this by our refusal to hate or to hurt others, by our liberality and generosity and by our love for <u>all</u> people, even those who act toward us with animosity and hatred. That is the goal toward which we move. It is an ideal which we can only in part ever attain. But in the words of the poet, Robert Browning, "Our reach must exceed our grasp, or what's a heaven for?" It is the goal toward which we strive. As St. Paul wrote to the Philippians: "Not that I ...am already perfect, but I press on to make it my own...forgetting what lies behind and straining forward to what lies ahead I press on toward the goal..."(Phil. 3:12-14) That is the aim which Jesus empowers us to pursue. Not in some other world, but in this one, here and now!

Last Sunday After the Epiphany
(The Transfiguration)

The Holy Mountain
and the Valley Below

Matthew 17:1-9

> *After six days Jesus took with him Peter and James and John his brother, and led them up a high mountain apart. And he was transfigured before them, and his face shone like the sun, and his garments became white as light. And behold, there appeared to them Moses and Elijah, talking with him. And Peter said to Jesus, "Lord, it is well that we are here; if you wish, I will make three booths here, one for you and one for Moses and one for Elijah." He was still speaking, when lo, a bright cloud overshadowed them, and a voice from the cloud said, "This is my beloved Son, with whom I am well pleased; listen to him." When the disciples heard this, they fell on their faces, and were filled with awe. But Jesus came and touched them, saying, "Rise, and have no fear." And when they lifted up their eyes, they saw no one but Jesus only. And as they were coming down the mountain, Jesus commanded them, "Tell no one the vision, until the Son of man is raised from the dead."*

The events described in this text left a deep and lasting impression on the three disciples who were present. In the 2nd Epistle attributed to Peter, the writer states, "We did not follow cleverly devised myths when we made known to you the power and coming of our Lord Jesus Christ, but we were eyewitnesses of His majesty...for we were with him on the holy mountain". And the result of this experience was that, "We have the prophetic word made more sure." Then he spells out its lesson for his readers, "You will do well to pay attention to this (word) as to a lamp shining in a dark place..."(2 Peter 1:16-19) The vision of Jesus' transfiguration on the 'holy mountain' remained always for Peter, James and John a 'bright and shining hour'. These brief moments of revelation retained their inspiration for a lifetime.

Each of us have known situations which while perhaps not similar in degree or intensity, may still rightfully be called 'mountain-top' experiences. In these moments the dark clouds of doubt and fear have scurried away, and the bright light of faith and hope have filled our hearts to overflowing, and we have exclaimed with Peter, "Lord it is well that we are here."

This transfiguration of dull reality into the mystical vision that uplifts and inspires can happen at anytime. It may take place as we read the Scripture, or pray, or listen to the preaching of the Word. But the 'mountain top' experience is not in any way confined to these so called 'religious' activities. It may come to us at our work-place, in our home, our car, or on a sick bed. It may appear in the smile of a child, or the consoling word of a friend, or in the remembrance of a deceased loved one. It may happen as we listen to a bird's song, or gaze up at the stars, or admire the beauty of a flower. There is no limit as to how and where it can happen. We do not control the time or the place when we may be transported in the twinkling of an eye to the 'mountain-top'. But having been there, we never forget it. And these moments, though fragile and fleeting and mysterious, may prove more real and precious to us than all the others. They are not to be rationalized but received with gratitude. Then in the difficult and dreary days that fill up the greater part of our life, we can remember and call them to mind, and like Peter, let them inspire us and increase our willingness to listen to God's word and act on it. In times of doubt and despair, when our faith falters, we can call again to mind those precious moments. They are like money in the bank. We can draw on them whenever the need arises.

Yet however comforting and uplifting these moments of transfiguration may be, God never intends them as an end in themselves. On the holy mountain Peter expressed his willingness to build three booths, one for Jesus, and one each for Moses and Elijah. His purpose is not clear. Whatever the reason for his words, the building of booths indicated a desire to remain there for a time, to prolong the experience. But Peter's intentions were interrupted by a voice which said, "This is my beloved Son, in whom I am well pleased. Listen to him". Peter could not help but have been reminded of words Jesus spoke to the disciples just before the Transfiguration. He told them that he must endure suffering and death, and that they were to take up their cross and follow in his footsteps. Peter and the others had found these words difficult to accept. They did not want to hear them. But now they are told to listen! The hard duties and demands of life were still calling.

Then Jesus led his disciples down from the mountain to the valley below, and we are directly transported from this scene of mystic rapture to the pitiful cries of a convulsed child, coupled with the anguished pleas of his father. It is significant that immediately following the account of the Transfiguration the writer of Matthew describes the pathetic and baffling spectacle of an epileptic child in need of healing and help. What a drastic descent from the exhilarating heights of a moving spiritual experience to the disconcerting ills and demands of real life. On the night before he was killed, Martin Luther King,Jr. delivered an impassioned speech in which he exclaimed to his listeners that he had been to the mountain-top and like Moses had looked out over the promised land. He had been granted the vision of a future blessed time yet to come. But the very next morning it was back to the battle of fighting for decent wages and working conditions for the garbage workers, with the deadly danger it involved.

Jesus did not come into this world to lift us out of it or above it, or to shelter us from its valleys of despair nor its garbage dumps of injustice. He came into this world to give us a vision of what life is meant to be and can in part become. He came into this world to equip us with the strength and love we need to live in the world and for it. Jesus did not ignore the plight of the epileptic. He ministered to the child. He was able to bring healing, and intimated that we also have the power to bring needed help to others, if we only believe.

It comes down to this. Our devotional life must never be separated from our daily life. Spirituality and social concern are not separate entities, but integrated aspects of the full and abundant life which Jesus came to bring. Like Peter, we have misunderstood the meaning of worship if we look to its soaring moments of inspiration as ends in themselves. Worship is not intended as an escape, but as an equipment for life. Its goal is not simply to comfort but also to challenge. It is not a place of refuge from the world, but a place of renewal for involvement in it. That is why the liturgy of the Church closes with the phrase, "Go in peace. Serve the Lord."

Karl Marx once criticized organized religion by claiming that it was the "opiate of the people". The drug of primary use in his day was opium. Today it's crack or cocaine. What Marx was really saying is that when we use religion to realize a kind of 'spiritual high' that allows us to ignore the troubles of the world, because everything feels all right inside, because we have Jesus in our hearts and heaven as our home, then we have employed religion to escape the hurt and pain and turmoil of the world. In one of John Edgar Wideman's books, an addict explains why he turned to drugs. The "world was a hurting trick and being high was being out of the world...Whoever said you supposed to just stand still and suffer? No. You take the freedom train running through your veins." We are learning more every day what a terrible personal price there is to pay for this kind of flight. The attempt to escape pain becomes in the end a living hell. We are learning too, that each of us, our entire society, pays a horrendous price for its escape from the cost of seeking social justice. We are learning that unemployment and underemployment, homelessness, lack of medical care and the resulting loss of hope, exacts a terrible toll on everyone in our society.

All the more reason then that we steadfastly resist the temptation to use religion as a drug, a freedom train, to escape from life. It is understandable that as the problems pile higher and solutions appear less feasible, we feel like flying away to some safe haven, to our own little personal mountain- top. But Jesus wants us to do what we can where we are, with whatever ability we have been given. The real purpose of our worship is to strengthen the weak knees and the trembling hands, to stand us on our feet again and send us into a hurting world, that we might hold out to others the gift of healing and help, however small, that God has placed in our hands and in our heart.

Jesus' Temptations and Ours

Matthew 4:1-11

> Then Jesus was led up by the Spirit into the wilderness to be tempted by the devil. And he fasted forty days and forty nights, and afterward he was hungry. And the tempter came and said to him, "If you are the Son of God, command these stones to become loaves of bread." But he answered, "It is written, 'Man shall not live by bread alone, but by every word that proceeds from the mouth of God.'" Then the devil took him to the holy city, and set him on the pinnacle of the temple, and said to him, "If you are the Son of God, throw yourself down; for it is written, 'He will give his angels charge of you,' and 'On their hands they will bear you up, lest you strike your foot against a stone.'" Jesus said to him, "Again it is written, 'You shall not tempt the Lord your God.'" Again, the devil took him to a very high mountain, and showed him all the kingdoms of the world and the glory of them; and he said to him, "All these I will give you, if you will fall down and worship me." Then Jesus said to him, "Begone, Satan! for it is written, 'You shall worship the Lord your God and him only shall you serve.'" Then the devil left him, and behold, angels came and ministered to him.

To be human is to know temptation. Since Jesus was fully human, his experiences were similar to our own. The three temptations recorded by Matthew in this text cannot possibly include the entire gamut of those which Jesus faced during his life. Neither do they cover in detail the multitudinous forms of temptation that each of us confront under vastly dissimilar circumstances. Yet we can be assured that they contain the essence of the temptations with which we struggle, as well as the strategies by which they can most effectively be resisted.

At the outset we note that Jesus was "led by the spirit into the wilderness to be tempted by the devil." This does not mean that the Spirit of God actually tempts us, but it does imply that God allows and may actually guide us into situations where temptations are likely if not inevitable. It is true that Jesus taught us to pray that we not be led "into temptation" and that is a needful prayer, for temptations are deadly dangerous. But it's a prayer that cannot always be answered. It was after Jesus was tempted that "angels came and ministered to him." While temptations have the potential to weaken or even destroy us, we are never stronger than when we have faced them and prevailed. Robert Browning described it this way, "...When the fight begins within himself, a man's worth something. God stoops o'er his head, Satan looks up between his feet- both tug- He's left himself, i' the middle: the soul wakes and grows."

The first of Jesus ordeals is described in this way. "The tempter said... to him, 'If you are the Son of God command these stones to be made bread.'" In essence, Jesus is here tempted to divorce himself from his complete identification with the human life. The hunger for bread represents here all of the wants and needs of a suffering humanity. Jesus is determined to experience fully the pain of physical hunger which then and now pervades the lives of the majority of people in this world. He voluntarily chose to identify himself first and foremost with the hungry, poor, and oppressed. In this world so unjustly divided between the powerful and the weak, the rich and the poor, he chose to remain in close communion with those who are forced to do without even the bare necessities of life. His action calls us to resist the temptation to hoard the resources with which we have been blessed. The fasting that has been a traditional part of the Christian observance of Lent is one small way in which to identify with hunger. It is only as we discover ways to empathize with those less fortunate than ourselves that we are inspired to feed the hungry, to clothe the naked, to visit the sick and the lonely, rather than to simply satisfy our own personal desires.

Jesus answer to this temptation is significant. His reply, as in each of the others, is a direct quotation from the Scripture contained in the book of Deuteronomy. "Man shall not live by bread alone, but by every word that proceeds from the mouth of God." (Deut. 8:3) Bread is a primary necessity for this earthly life. It is essential but it is not sufficient in itself. Life is more. When we have bread enough and to spare, life consists in sharing it. The life abundant, which Jesus came to provide, consists in loving our neighbor as ourself. Today when millions of people in Eastern Europe and the former Soviet Union face economic collapse with its consequent hardships, the call goes out to fall down and worship the golden calf of free enterprise and capitalism with its glittering promises of larger bank accounts, plenty of food, bigger cars and fancier clothes. But once possessed these things quickly turn to dust in one's hands, while the spirit is left empty and the heart hollow. We cannot live without bread, but neither can we live by bread alone.

Next we are told that the devil transported Jesus to Jerusalem, where he placed him high up on a pinnacle of the Temple and directed him to cast himself down, quoting somewhat imprecisely the promise that God "will give his angels charge of you," and "On their hands they will bear you up, lest you dash your foot against a stone." (Ps. 91:11-12) It is obvious that all of the temptations recorded in this text, are not to be understood as having literally transpired. But the devil's dare to jump off the tower of the Temple, represents a type of temptation that was very real in the life of Jesus and in our own as well. It is the temptation to escape in a reckless or irresponsible manner from reality, from duty, or from suffering, while piously placing everything, including our own destiny, in the hands of God. This was the kind of temptation that came to its climax for Jesus in the Garden of Gethsemane where we read that sweat oozed from his pores like drops of blood, and he prayed, "If it be possible, let this cup pass from me." (Matt. 26:39) Throughout his life Jesus was continually enticed to take the mad leap down and away from his calling, to escape the pain and agony of the cross. Even as he was being crucified, he was tempted in the same way. Those who passed by called out to him, "Save yourself. If you are the Son of God, come down from the Cross."(Matt. 27:40)

79

This temptation to escape from the heart-rending realities and duties of life is one from which we are never quite free. We are tempted to run from the complex and overwhelming problems of our earthly existence. "Stop the world, I want to get off" may seem only a fanciful line, but it is often a very apt description of the way we really feel. This desire is expressed in countless ways in literature and song. It is the cry of the Psalmist "Oh if I had the wings of a dove, I would fly away and be at rest." (Psalm 55:6) Jesus saw clearly that to indulge in this flight, while piously placing oneself in the care of God, was a perversion of Scripture. So he answered the devil with another passage, "You shall not tempt the Lord your God."(Deut. 6:16)

To give up, to stop trying, to write off the world and its problems, because the task seems hopeless, or costly, or dangerous, is in reality to give up on God. This is true, even when we rationalize our loss of hope under the guise of religion. It is true even when we quote Scripture to the effect that God will take care of everything, that His Kingdom is not 'of this world'. The Devil keeps on whispering in our ear, "Jump down from the cross. Quit trying. God will save you and take you to heaven. That's all that matters." But God has given us a life to live, abilities to use, a world to care for and improve.

The last temptation of Jesus is perhaps the most formidable of all. The devil showed Jesus all the kingdoms of the world and their glory, and said to him, "All these I will give to you, if you will fall down and worship me." Here the tempter holds before Jesus the lure of worldly power and position, at the price of compromising his own inner convictions and beliefs. In Faustian fashion Jesus is enticed to 'sell his soul' to the devil. In practice, Jesus could have expressed this homage to Satan by toning down his criticism of the religious authorities, by buttering them up rather than dressing them down, by pandering to their prejudices and perversion of the Scriptures, by being a reformer rather than a revolutionary. He could have healed people on other days than the Sabbath, confined His teachings to the poor, rather than offending the rich and the powerful. He could have rationalized that the best way to change things over the long haul was to be patient and

80

prudent, to use gentle persuasion rather than aggressive confrontation. But crucial convictions would have been compromised and truth trampled in the dust.

The temptation to compromise with evil confronts each of us daily. We are scarcely free from it for a moment. It is the key to worldly power, popularity, wealth, and advancement. On the one hand it must be frankly admitted that to some degree compromise is necessary. It is not only essential to life, but can result in the accomplishment of much that is good. Politicians must reach compromises to pass needed legislation. Husband and wife must compromise in order to live in peace. In this sense compromise comprises a practical program for progress. The real test lies in learning to distinguish which convictions are crucial and which can be at least partially sacrificed to obtain some greater good. Jesus perceived that the price he had to pay was in this instance far too great. It meant bowing down to the devil, it meant deserting a major purpose of his life.

No one of us is exempt from this temptation anymore than Jesus. Unlike Jesus, we do not always win the battle. Sometimes our knowledge is not sufficient or our courage is not adequate. But the example of Jesus and his identification with our predicament and our struggle is a mighty source of strength. As the writer of the letter to the Hebrews put it, "we have not a high priest who is unable to sympathize with our weaknesses, but one who in every respect has been tempted as we are, yet without sinning. Let us then with confidence draw near to the throne of grace, that we may receive mercy and find grace to help in time of need." (Heb. 4:15-16)

With this help we can learn to say more and more often in the time of temptation, "Begone Satan, for it is written, 'You shall worship the Lord your God, and him only shall you serve.'" (Deut. 6:13) And when we are able to do that, then our strength is renewed and enlarged. It is as if angels come and minister to us!

2nd Sunday In Lent

Worship God In Spirit and Truth

John 4:5-10; 15-30; 39-42

> *So he came to a city of Samaria called Sychar, near the field that Jacob gave to his son Joseph. Jacob's well was there, and so Jesus, wearied as he was with his journey, sat down beside the well. It was about the sixth hour. There came a woman of Samaria to draw water. Jesus said to her, "Give me a drink." For his disciples had gone away into the city to buy food. The Samaritan woman said to him, "How is it that you, a Jew ask a drink of me, a woman of Samaria?", for Jews have no dealings with Samaritans. Jesus answered her, "If you knew the gift of God, and who it is that is saying to you," 'give me a drink,' you would have asked him, and he would have given you living water." The woman said to him, "Sir, you have nothing to draw with, and the well is deep; where do you get that living water? Are you greater than our father Jacob, who gave us the well, and drank from it himself, and his sons, and his cattle?" Jesus said to her, "Every one who drinks of this water will thirst again, but whoever drinks of the water that I shall give him will never thirst; the water that I shall give him will become in him a spring of water welling up to eternal life." The woman said to him, "Sir, give me this water, that I may not thirst, nor come here to draw." … Jesus said to her, "Go, call your husband, and come here." The woman answered him, "I have no husband." Jesus said to her, "You are right in saying, 'I have no husband'; for you have had five husbands, and he whom you now have is not your husband; this you said truly." The woman said to him, "Sir, I perceive that you are a prophet. Our fathers worshiped on this mountain; and you say that in Jerusalem is the place where men ought to worship." Jesus*

said to her, "Woman, believe me, the hour is coming when neither on this mountain nor in Jerusalem will you worship the Father. You worship what you do not know; we worship what we know, for salvation is from the Jews. But the hour is coming, and now is, when the true worshipers will worship the Father in spirit and truth, for such the Father seeks to worship him. God is spirit, and those who worship him must worship him in spirit and truth." The woman said to him, "I know that Messiah is coming (he who is called Christ); when he comes, he will show us all things." Jesus said to her, "I who speak to you am he." Just then his disciples came. They marveled that he was talking with a woman, but none said, "What do you wish?" or, "Why are you talking with her?" So the woman left her water jar, and went away into the city, and said to the people, "Come, see a man who told me all that I ever did. Can this be the Christ?" They went out of the city and were coming to him. ... Many Samaritans from that city believed in him because of the woman's testimony, "He told me all that I ever did." So when the Samaritans came to him, they asked him to stay with them; and he stayed there two days. And many more believed because of his word. They said to the woman, "It is no longer because of your words that we believe, for we have heard for ourselves, and we know that this is indeed the Savior of the world."

The text records a long conversation between Jesus and a Samaritan woman. The strange thing is that it took place at all. Jewish teachers were forbidden to talk with women, especially in any kind of protracted discussion of a religious nature. We know from numerous other references in the Gospels that Jesus paid little attention to this sexist taboo. While none of the twelve were women, some of his closest friends were, and also many of his most devoted followers. This particular conversation must have been one of Jesus' earliest contacts, for the text states that the disciples "marvelled that he was talking with a woman."(v. 27) The woman herself was doubly surprised because as she was quick to point out, Jews had "no dealings with Samaritans".(v. 9) The hostility between Jews and Samaritans was centuries old and fueled by the fires of controversy over conflicting religious convictions. For reasons delineated in the 17th chapter of 2 Kings, the Jews looked upon the Samaritan religion as a perverse mixture of both truth and falsehood, and refused to have any dealings with them. One of the most heated points of their controversy centered on the Samaritans rejection of the Temple in Jerusalem as the primary and most holy place of worship. The Samaritans, had erected their own Temple on Mt. Gerizim, close by the well where Jesus and the woman conversed. While the Temple itself had been destroyed, the Samaritans still worshipped there, and this was considered by most Jews as a blasphemous act and outright rejection of God.

Jesus simply ignored this human created chasm of doctrinal difference. So when the Samaritan woman approached the well where Jesus sat resting he asked her to give him a drink. Without knowledge of the circumstances, this might appear a trivial and superficial request. In reality it was both unusual and significant. Drinking or eating together were acts that symbolized a close communion, and Jesus request indicated his willingness to drink from her cup or vessel, since he had none of his own.(v.11) The result was a lengthy and fruitful discussion of a deeply personal and spiritual nature. The woman felt free to openly discuss their religious differences. In the end she was so profoundly impressed by Jesus that she brought many of her friends to talk with him. As a consequence he stayed with them two whole days and many Samaritans were convinced that he was the Savior of the world.(v. 42) What an uplifting story to ponder, as we contemplate the devastating hostilities which separate us from one another in our world today.

The true purpose of religion is here displayed. Our faith in God is intended to draw people together in the realization of their common humanity and needs. Yet in many instances it seems to exacerbate differences rather than heal them, or even to serve as the source of alienation. In many areas of our world we are still confronted with these deep-seated and deadly divisions. Jesus spoke to the Samaritan woman in spite of all the cultural, political and religious reasons for simply sitting there with his lips tightly closed. His act punctuates the power of communication and the possibilities it presents for overcoming divisions. He only said "Give me a drink". But it was a start, and the results exceeded anyone's expectations.

When Israeli's say, "We cannot talk to Palestinians because we believe that they advocate violence," or when white South African conservatives say the same about their black counter-parts in the African National Congress, then the possibilities for reconciliation are practically nullified. When this happens anywhere in the world, the result is the same. When it occurs in the family, when wife says to husband, or husband to wife, "Don't talk to me." or "I don't want to talk about it," then the problems are perpetuated. Talking with another person in spite of drastic disagreements or seemingly insurmountable obstacles, is healing in itself. It is the opening of the door of possibility. It literally forces one human being to look into the face of another and see there a reflection of his or her own self. The willingness to talk is in itself an act of acceptance and of respect for the other person. It is the bed-rock essential for any resolution of human conflict. Once an open and sincere conversation begins, there is no way to anticipate what may happen. There are no limits to the differences that may be resolved, nor to the insight and understanding which may unfold.

The conversation which ensued between Jesus and the Samaritan woman provides an explicit example. Here are two people that might have passed like ships in the night, estranged by their nationality and religion, remaining forever strangers and foes. But as they reach out to one another in conversation, some unexpected things happen. Jesus speaks about giving the woman "living water...welling up to eternal life". Then he reveals that he is aware of some very intimate matters regarding her personal life; namely, that she has had five husbands and that she is not married to the man with whom she now lives. The woman is deeply impressed, not only by Jesus' knowledge, but by his attitude. He has not lectured to her or pronounced judgment on her way of life or her religion. Instead he has offered her some sort of mysterious gift, and accepted her as a person. At this point the woman feels free to broach directly the delicate subject of the religious beliefs which divide Samaritans from Jews. The conversation has moved all the way from a casual request for a drink of water, to the most essential concerns of faith and life. "Our fathers worshipped on this mountain", the woman states, looking up at Mt. Gerizim, "and you say that in Jerusalem is the place where men ought to worship." And Jesus reply contains a profound and revolutionary declaration of the faith he came to reveal, "Woman, believe me", he said, "the hour is coming when neither on this mountain nor in Jerusalem will you worship the Father"..."The hour is coming and now is, when the true worshippers will worship the Father in spirit and in truth...God is Spirit and those who worship him must worship in spirit and truth."(v. 20-24)

There is more here than any of us can fully comprehend, and this was true for the Samaritan woman as well; but there is enough that we can understand to throw important light on a key element of the Christian faith. Jesus here declares that the matter which had divided Samaritans and Jews over the centuries, as to the primary place where God could be properly worshipped, was of no real consequence. Both sides were wrong. Their basic concern misguided and misdirected. The essential thing is not the place where one worships, nor any of the various liturgical rites or symbols connected with particular places or groups of believers. It is not the geographical location or the form of worship that has importance, but its object and the manner in which it is consummated. No one place can be designated as primary for worship over any other. God is Spirit, available in the same degree to all people in all places. God is like the wind that blows where it wills(3:8), not confined to any Temple or place or ritual practice. "The most High does not dwell in houses made with hands."(Acts 7:47) God is the spirit that Jesus came into this world to reveal in its flesh and blood reality, the Spirit of light and of love, the spirit of justice and of righteousness. It is that universal Spirit, which is the object of all true worship.

Jesus directive to worship God in spirit does not refer to prayer or worship divorced from the flesh and blood realities of this world. On the contrary, it means that worship, to be real, must be expressed in the Spirit of the God who became incarnate. To worship God in spirit is to love God and to love our neighbor as ourself. This is all that God requires of us. St. Paul describes "spiritual worship" in terms of presenting our "bodies as a living sacrifice"(Romans 12:1) and this sacrifice is manifested in a love that is genuine, in holding fast to what is good, and in loving one another with brotherly affection.(Romans 12:9)

Our worship is to be not only in spirit, but also in truth. It is not the symbols and forms utilized by Samaritans and Jews, Protestants and Catholics, Christians and Muslims, that contain the essentials of worship. We spend a lot of wasted time and effort arguing over which eucharistic formula or which liturgical garb or which form of worship is most correct or effective. Real worship of the one Lord and Creator of all, is that which is performed in truth, without hypocrisy or deceit, with the honesty and conviction which leads to sincere confession of our common creaturehood and the resolute determination to express our gratitude in actual deeds of love for our neighbor, especially to the "least of these", the poor and the oppressed.

What a glorious proclamation! What a welcome deliverance from the petty divisions that set us in opposition to one another! God is Spirit, freely available to all people. Worship God in spirit and in truth! The word of Jesus to the woman of Samaria breaks down the walls that separate us from each other. It pulls people together in a common worship which leads to a fuller expression of love and justice. No wonder the Samaritan woman was impressed! No wonder she brought her friends to Jesus and that many of them followed him too. Jesus has entrusted that identical message to us and if we deliver it in person, the results can be the same!

3rd Sunday In Lent

Work While It Is Day

John 9:1-17 & 34-39

       As he (Jesus) passed by, he saw a man blind from his birth. And his disciples asked him, "Rabbi, who sinned, this man or his parents, that he was born blind?" Jesus answered, "It was not that this man sinned, or his parents, but that the works of God might be made manifest in him. We must work the works of him who sent me, while it is day; night comes, when no one can work. As long as I am in the world, I am the light of the world." As he said this, he spat on the ground and made clay of the spittle and anointed the man's eyes with the clay, saying to him, "Go, wash in the pool of Siloam" (which means Sent). So he went and washed and came back seeing. The neighbors and those who had seen him before as a beggar, said, "Is not this the man who used to sit and beg?" Some said, "It is he"; others said, "no, but he is like him." He said, "I am the man." They said to him, "Then how were your eyes opened?" He answered, "The man called Jesus made clay and anointed my eyes and said to me, 'Go to Siloam and wash'; so I went and washed and received my sight." They said to him, "Where is he?" He said, "I do not know.

       "They brought to the Pharisees the man who had formerly been blind. Now it was a sabbath day when Jesus made the clay and opened his eyes. The Pharisees again asked him how he had received his sight. And he said to them, "He put clay on my eyes, and I washed, and I see." Some of the Pharisees said, "This man is not from God, for he does not keep the sabbath." But others said, "How can a man who is a sinner do such signs?" There was a division among them. So they again said to the blind man, "What do

you say about him, since he has opened your eyes?"
He said, "He is a prophet."

> *...They answered him, "You were born in utter sin, and would you teach us?" And they cast him out. Jesus heard that they had cast him out, and having found him he said, "Do you believe in the Son of man?" He answered, "And who is he, sir, that I may believe in him?" Jesus said to him, "You have seen him, and it is he who speaks to you." He said, "Lord, I believe"; and he worshiped him. Jesus said, "For judgment I came in to this world, that those who do not see may see, and that those who see may become blind." Some of the Pharisees near him heard this, and they said to him, "Are we also blind?" Jesus said to them, "If you were blind, you would have no guilt; but now that you say, 'We see', your guilt remains."*

Time and again the Gospel of John portrays Jesus as the one who came into the world to shed light upon the darkness which surrounds us, to cure our blindness, to help us see and understand the truth, so that we might live according to it.

This entire 9th chapter of John's Gospel is given over to a remarkable and insightful story of how Jesus restored the vision of a man who had been blind from birth. What interested the disciples about this man was the question of why he had entered into life shackled with such a terrible affliction. They shared a rather common belief that every instance of disease or disaster was directly traceable to some specific sin. And so they asked Jesus, "Rabbi, who sinned, this man or his parents, that he was born blind?" How an infant could at the moment of birth reap the reward of someone else's sin is difficult to conceive. But the point is that Jesus disciples were concerned here with a religious question. In essence they wanted to know <u>who</u> was responsible for this affliction. Who or what caused it to happen?

In a somewhat different form, this is still the query that we most often raise in the face of suffering and sorrow. <u>Why</u> did it happen, and why did it happen to me, or to him or her? It is a highly theoretical question, which is really impossible to answer with any degree of certitude. It is understandable, however, that the question persists. We would like to have a definite answer. And so we give answers, on our own. We blame ourselves, or other people,. We blame the devil. We blame God. But these answers are based, for the most part, on pure conjecture. They do not really satisfy the basic feeling we express in asking the question. This universal human cry of 'Why did it happen?', is at heart a lament that it should happen at <u>all</u>. It is a protest against unexplained tragedy, an unwillingness or inability to accept the evil and suffering that fills our world and sometimes overwhelms us.

Too often we are content to utilize religion and theology in a futile attempt to answer the unanswerable. When this happens, then in effect, religion is being used as an escape mechanism. It is confined to dealing with the abstract and the abstruse. It deals with what might have been, or what should have been, or what will be, rather than what <u>is</u>. It muses about why things may have happened or what caused them to happen instead of prescribing what can be done with things as they are, where they <u>are</u>. When this occurs, then religion has deteriorated into 'pious drivel', into 'talk' for 'talk's sake', into a fanciful flight from earthly realities.

Jesus answer to the disciples brings their hypothetical questions back down to earth. "It was not that this man sinned, or his parents, but that the works of God might be made manifest in him."(v.3) Jesus not only rejects the disciples theories about the possible causes of the man's blindness; he ignores, and in effect, rejects the question itself as unanswerable and therefore worthless. In stating that this affliction is for the purpose of manifesting the works of God, he does not speculate as to the cause of the blindness. He rather indicates how it is to be accepted and used. So the question for us is not where suffering has come from or why, but what we are to do with it. It is to be employed for the purpose of bringing about some good in the world.

Jesus directs us to lay aside our resentful speculations about the origin of our sorrows and tragedies. His advice is clear and concise and practical, "We must work the works of him who sent me, while it is day; night comes when no one can work." (v.4)

Indeed, the day is extremely short, and comes swiftly to its close. The little time we have been given to live and breathe upon this earth, is not to be wasted in idle speculations, even though they may be clothed in the pompous language of religion. Neither is the faith God has placed in our hearts to be misused in vain attempts to penetrate those mysterious regions which lie forever beyond our human vision.

The world is the place that God has put us for this fleeting yet portentous time. It is possible that we are being shaped for some mysterious and wondrous future, more glorious than we can grasp or even imagine. But Christ came to help us through this life and this world. There is no more high nor holy purpose for our lives then the one he bestows upon us here and now, 'to work the work of God, while it is still day'.

William Watson put it this way in his poem, "The Hope of the World":

"Let me learn...on this world no more to cast ignoble slight,
Counting it but the door of other worlds more bright.
Here, where I fail or conquer, here is my concern."

It is not in flights of fancy or speculation, nor in dreams of greater worlds to come or of a brighter future on a farther shore, that Christ calls us to work the works of God. No, rather he says, "As long as I am in the world, I am the light of the world" and having said that he spit on the ground, and taking up the moistened clay, from which we all come, he placed it on the blind man's eyes, and gave him back his sight. Christ used the material of the earth to do the work of God in the world. And he calls us to do the same. He directs us to the duty which lies nearest us. He beckons us to reach out in love to those whose needs confront us. Christ does not ask us to disown our limitations or bemoan our sufferings, but to use them. He echoed the words of the Preacher who proclaimed long before, "Whatever your hand finds to do, do it with your whole might".(Ecc. 9:10)

Several years ago a woman in California unknowingly contracted the AIDS virus through a blood transfusion. Unaware of the peril, she passed it on through breast feeding to her two children. Within a relatively short time one of the children succumbed to the dread disease. Both the mother and the surviving child now faced the possibility of the same fate. This woman could have spent whatever time remained to her, lamenting her fate or her bad luck, or blaming the devil or God, wrestling over and over with the inexplicable and self-defeating question of 'why' it had to happen. Instead, she determined to do whatever she could to fight the battle against AIDS, particularly as it affects little children, thousands of whom have been infected and many of whom have already died. She organized a group in her home state to raise money for research. She testified before a Congressional Committee on AIDS as to the urgent need for more funding, care facilities and study. In an interview, she was asked how she managed to face her personal and family tragedy with such courage. Her reply was that on the death of her child, she realized that she had only two basic alternatives. Either she could give up and do nothing, or she could use each day she still remained alive to do what she was able in order to help others in situations similar to her own. By doing this she could also help herself and her child.

Those of us who are willing and able to follow that example, even in the smallest fraction of a degree, have been cured of our blindness as surely as the man whom Jesus healed in this text. With that man, we can say, "Once I was blind, but now I see." The worst kind of blindness is not physical but spiritual. There are those, who like the Pharisees are blind but don't even know it, who have eyes but cannot see.

Thank God for the gift of a vision that enables us to see in this world, here in what Thomas Carlyle described as "this poor, miserable, despicable, Actual", with all its sin and evil and suffering, the only place we have to work out our "salvation with fear and trembling".(Phil.2:12) Thank God for eyes that can see and treasure the tremendous insight contained in Jesus' words, "Work...while it is day; night comes, when no one can work".

4th Sunday In Lent

True Greatness

Matthew 20:17-28

> *As Jesus was going up to Jersalem, he took the twelve disciples aside, and on the way he said to them, "Behold, we are going up to Jerusalem; and the Son of man will be delivered to the chief priests and scribes, and they will condemn him to death, and deliver him to the Gentiles to be mocked and scourged and crucified, and he will be raised on the third day."*
>
> *Then the mother of the sons of Zebedee came up to him, with her sons, and kneeling before him she asked him for something. And he said to her, "What do you want?" She said to him, "Command that these two sons of mine may sit, one at your right hand and one at your left, in your kingdom." But Jesus answered, "You do no know what you are asking. Are you able to drink the cup that I am to drink?" They said to him, "We are able." He said to them, "You will drink my cup, but to sit at my right hand and at my left is not mine to grant, but it is for those for whom it has been prepared by my Father." And when the ten heard it, they were indignant at the two brothers. But Jesus called them to him and said, "You know that the rulers of the Gentiles lord it over them, and their great men exercise authority over them. It shall not be so among you; but whoever would be great among you must be your servant, and whoever would be first among you must be your slave; even as the Son of man came not to be served but to serve, and to give his life as a ransom for many."*

In this text Jesus teaches his disciples and us about the meaning of true greatness. The words were spoken as they traveled toward Jerusalem. Jesus explains to the disciples that upon their arrival the chief priests and scribes would connive to have him arrested. Then he would be condemned and crucified as a criminal, and afterwards raised from the dead. As he concluded speaking he was approached by the mother of James and John. She brought her sons in tow, and begged from Jesus a favor. "Command that these two sons of mine may sit, one at your right hand and one at your left, in your kingdom." She is typical of many parents who desire the best for their children. They want them to have the best education, the best schools, the best jobs, the best salaries. They want their children to succeed. Even though this mother's sons were fully grown and quite capable of speaking for themselves, she takes the lead, and intercedes on their behalf.

Jesus does not reprimand her, but directs his answer to the disciples themselves. The request for the highest places of honor and power in the kingdom Jesus has come to inaugurate, involves something far different from what they or their mother envision. So he says, "You do not know what you are asking." They had apparently misunderstood what he has just told them, that his path was leading to persecution and suffering and death. So he inquires, "Are you able to drink the cup that I am to drink?" Without hesitation they answer, "We are able." They had their eyes on the prize and the price to be paid in terms of any hardship or suffering seemed small in comparison. They were supremely confident. They were up to the task.

Jesus takes them at their word. He realizes that even though they cannot comprehend at this time the sharpness of the sorrows, nor the depth of the pain that they will be called to endure, yet they will indeed share in these sufferings. "You will drink from my cup", he says. That part is true. "But to sit at my right hand and at my left is not mine to grant,... but it is for those for whom it has been prepared by my Father."

It is easy to misinterpret this statement. This is no ascription of an aimless or arbitrary power on the part of God, as if the places of honor in the kingdom were assigned by choices as random as the roll of dice, or picking a lottery number out of a bowl. The inheritance of divinely reserved places of honor depends on meeting the requirements of true greatness. Everything hinges on the definition of 'greatness'. The 'greatness' which Jesus describes cannot be granted by request. It is not the result of ambition nor is it a matter of favoritism. It is reserved for those who love and serve their Creator in their fellow human beings, who pay the price of a faith which is active in love. It is not something we can demand or earn, but something that is automatically inherited by those who enter the ranks of discipleship, who live a life of service to others.

Now when the other ten disciples heard what Jesus was saying and realized what was being requested, "they were indignant at the two brothers". They were angry, and their hostility arose from the fact that they shared the same desire as James and John, but had not been forward enough or aggressive enough to express it. They too, were eager to attain the places of honor at Jesus side. They had the same misconception as to the meaning of greatness. They were jealous. Now, if we hold to a kind of otherworldly view of religion we might be somewhat disillusioned by this, and say to ourselves, "Is it possible that this sort of in-fighting and bickering and competitiveness existed even among the disciples of our Lord? Of course it did! They were human beings, just like you and me. The driving ambition for power and prestige is an ingredient of the humanity which we all share. Whether we admit it or not, we all have a deep-set need for status. We would all like to have first place, be the favorite child, the head of the class, the honored guest, the star of the game. Whether consciously or not, we can all identify with the forthright phrase made famous by Mohammed Ali, "I am the greatest". Now Jesus recognizes this, for he knows what is in us. He knows us better than we know ourselves. Neither does he condemn our innate ambition and drive to be great, anymore than he did that of his disciples. He did not come into the world to condemn but to rescue and to save and to help.

So Jesus did not denounce the disciples desire, but caringly and patiently taught them what true greatness really involves. First he reminds them of what they already know. "You know that the rulers of the Gentiles lord it over them, and their great men exercise authority over them." That was the commonly held and accepted view of 'greatness'. It still holds sway today. Greatness is equated with power and the exercise of authority. Greatness is measured by the amount of wealth and material possessions accumulated. Greatness is gauged by the degrees you hold, or the type of work you do, or the authority you wield over the lives and fortunes of others. So the business man says, "I employ hundreds of people." Or the factory foreman says, "I have this many persons working under me." Or the husband talks about my wife and my family, or the clergy about his or her congregation.

The lust for a power and authority based primarily upon material wealth at the expense of any real commitment to global responsibility, is also hard at work in our present-day world. For nearly half a century the cold war's icy grip has frozen our resources in huge blocks of military hardware. Now at a time in history when a more peaceful co-existence appears at last within reach, a primary and universal question is being posed. Will the tremendous resources formerly devoted to producing weapons of war be utilized to serve the true and compelling needs of our world? Will they at long-last be used to serve humankind, to help alleviate poverty and illiteracy, and to provide health care and housing and other basic requirements for the most deprived and oppressed members of our global community? Will they be used to serve our earth, to save our environment from the stifling pollution of a technology devoted to material gain and greed?

The indicators are not all that promising. The countries of Eastern Europe, having cast aside oppressively authoritarian political regimes, appear to have their eyes fixated on the "golden calf" of capitalism with its promises of material and technological advancement. In the meantime, cultural, humane and environmental concerns are pushed to the side or forgotten altogether. It is vital that the churches of Eastern Europe who have provided a rallying place for the cry of 'freedom' do not now become an uncritical neutral observer of an obscene lust for power and economic control. What is truly important is not whether a government is capitalist or communist or socialist or something in between, but whether it functions to serve the real needs of its people, in particular those who are least powerful and most vulnerable to oppression of all kinds. When a government fails to do this, when a

98

portion of the people are degraded to the status of beggars, forced to plead for a dole so meager it scarcely sustains their existence, then it becomes imperative that Christian believers and the Church as the body of those believers, issue a strong and determined prophetic protest. This protest must take the form of a positive identification with those who are oppressed, and be carried out in the name and in the spirit of the one who came "to give his life as a ransom for many".(v. 28)

True greatness, as Jesus defined it, is the same for all, whether individual, family, church or nation. It is a kind of living shaped by concern. A living which has perceived that the highest goal is service rather than self-seeking, giving rather than taking. It is dedicated to sharing one's power on behalf of others rather than using one's power to rob others. It is not characterized by domination and control, but by decency and compassion and respect. It is a kind of living shaped after the pattern of One who came, "not to be served but to serve."(v.28)

Resurrection-Now

John 11:1-27

Now a certain man was ill, Lazarus of Bethany, the village of Mary and her sister Martha. It was Mary who anointed the Lord with ointment and wiped his feet with her hair, whose brother Lazarus was ill. So the sisters sent to him, saying, "Lord, he whom you love is ill." But when Jesus heard it he said, "This illness is not unto death; it is for the glory of God, so that the Son of God may be glorified by means of it."

Now Jesus loved Martha and her sister and Lazarus. So when he heard that he was ill, he stayed two days longer in the place where he was. Then after this he said to the disciples, "Let us go into Judea again." The disciples said to him, "Rabbi, the Jews were but now seeking to stone you, and are you going there again?" Jesus answered, "Are there not twelve hours in the day? If any one walks in the day, he does not stumble, because he sees the light of this world. But if any one walks in the night, he stumbles, because the light is not in him." Thus he spoke, and then he said to them, "Our friend Lazarus has fallen asleep, but I go to awake him out of sleep." The disciples said to him, "Lord, if he has fallen asleep, he will recover." Now Jesus had spoken of his death, but they thought that he meant taking rest in sleep. Then Jesus told them plainly, "Lazarus is dead; and for your sake I am glad that I was not there, so that you may believe. But let us go to him." Thomas, called the Twin, said to his fellow disciples, "Let us also go, that we may die with him."

Now when Jesus came, he found that Lazarus had already been in the tomb four days. Bethany was near Jerusalem, about two miles off, and many of the Jews had come to Martha and Mary to console them concerning their brother. When Martha heard that Jesus was coming, she went and met him, while Mary sat in the house. Martha said to Jesus, "Lord, if you had been here, my brother would not have died. And even now I know that whatever you ask from God, God will give you." Jesus said to her, "Your brother will rise again." Martha said to him "I know he will rise again in the resurrection at the last day." Jesus said to her, "I am the resurrection and the life; he who believes in me shall never die. Do you believe this?" She said to him, "Yes, Lord; I believe that you are the Christ, the Son of God, he who is coming into the world."

Jesus had a special relationship to the sisters Martha and Mary and their brother Lazarus. He often stayed in their home. The Scripture says that he loved them.(v.5) When Lazarus became ill and later died, Jesus was deeply grieved and when he saw the tomb where they had laid him, he wept.(v.35) What made Jesus decide to grant Lazarus a new lease on life? His personal feelings for both Lazarus and his bereaved sisters undoubtedly had something to do with it. But that appears not to have been the whole reason.

Jesus entire life and ministry was a witness to the power of God's spirit, a power to revive and lift up and give life. It was a witness to that spirit which the prophet Ezekiel proclaimed able to clothe dry bones once again with flesh and blood, and restore gladness and joy to those whose hope had been obliterated.(Ezekiel 37:11) The whole of Jesus teachings and actions conveyed a message of life where death prevailed.

In this world we are literally inundated with the reality of death. Death touches us in many shapes and forms. It torments us in the specter of self-doubt and fear and loneliness. The resulting apathy and loss of hope can result in a drastic withdrawal from life. It is a 'leukemia of the spirit' which sucks out the life-sustaining marrow of our bones and dries it up. That is why we often refer to depression as a 'living death.' That is why the effort to keep hope alive is really a prayer for resurrection. Death is not only the end of this earthly life. There is a <u>death in the midst of life.</u>

The New Testament bears witness to the truth that there is also <u>life in the midst of death.</u> Jesus described the purpose of his ministry in this precise way. "The blind receive their sight and the lame walk, lepers are cleansed and the deaf hear, and the dead are raised up and the poor have good news preached to them."(Matt.11:4-6) In this same vein, the author of John's Gospel wrote concerning Jesus, "In him was life and the life was the light of men."(1:4) And later Jesus is quoted as saying, "I came that they may have life, and have it abundantly."(10:10) The life which Jesus came to bring to us is, as was the case with Lazarus, a life in the here and now. It is a life that we can grasp hold of in the midst of death.

When Jesus met the grieving Martha and told her that her brother would rise again, she said to him, "I know that he will rise again in the resurrection at the last day."(v. 24) Belief in the resurrection of the dead was a commonly held belief among a significant portion of the Jewish community. This belief was a distinguishing mark of the Pharisees as over against the Sadducees.(Acts 23:8) But Jesus did not offer to Martha, nor does he offer to us, the conventional consolation of life at some far off time, in some other world. The life he brings to share with us is not marked "for future use only." It is not reserved for the 'hereafter'. It is available now. The resurrected life is present in the person and in the Spirit of Jesus. So he says to Martha, "I <u>am</u> the resurrection and the life." Not I will be, someday, somewhere, sometime, but, "I <u>am</u>."

Heaven and hell do not begin in some remote future time. They begin <u>now</u> and <u>here</u>. The question is not, Where <u>will</u> we spend eternity but where <u>are</u> we spending it? Through faith we have the foretaste of eternal life now. The testimony to this truth is proclaimed throughout the Scripture. Jesus prayed, "This <u>is</u> eternal life, that they know you the only true God, and Jesus Christ whom you have sent."(John 17:3) And in the lst Letter of John we read, "God gave us eternal life, and this life is in his Son. He who has the Son has life... I write this to you who believe in the name of the Son of God that you may know that you have eternal life."(I John 5:11-13). Too often our understanding of resurrection is either relegated to an event that happened a long time ago, or it is focused on a future experience. But we rob ourselves of its fullest meaning when we circumscribe and curtail it in this way.

The story is told of a family who once inherited a grand piano. This marvelous instrument stood in their living room, carefully dusted and polished and regularly tuned, but no one in the house could play it, except one small child, who could, if called upon, thump out a passable rendition of "Chopsticks". This magnificent instrument might have filled the whole house with glorious music, but all that was ever heard from it was one mediocre little tune, rather poorly played. How tragic! It is the kind of tragedy that occurs when we confine the promise of resurrection to the past or the future and fail to play it out in the present. The life available to us through faith is capable of filling our entire existence with a superb spiritual music. It is capable of endowing our lives with new hope, strength, courage, vitality and most of all love. How sad then if we only utilize it to play one little tune, telling us how, after we die, we will live on in heaven. It is sad, not because the hope of an after-life is something small or insignificant, but because we have failed to understand the importance of this life. We have failed to perceive the meaning of that perceptive little prayer, "Lord, help me to live before I die."

The real meaning of the story of Lazarus is resurrection now. The love and compassion and power of God is alive and available in the world. There are resources at hand which can enable us to break out of the tombs which entrap us, to break free from the death that engulfs us. Fear and despair and hopelessness can never have the last word. Death is swallowed up in victory, because by the Spirit of God we are able to take hold of life in the midst of death.

What happened to Lazarus after Jesus granted him a new life in this world? We don't know much, but we do know that his very existence became a powerful witness to the Christian faith. In the 12th chapter of John we learn that not only did the chief priests plot to put Jesus to death but that they "planned to put Lazarus also to death, because on account of him, many of the Jews were going away and believing in Jesus." (v:10,11) God gives us eternal life, not to hoard but to share with others in the world where we

104

live. Here lies the deepest challenge of the resurrected life that Christ grants to all who believe. It is to use that life in the present moment through actual deeds of kindness and compassion and concern, as a witness to God's love. Then it can be said of us as it was of Lazarus that "on account of him many...were believing in Jesus."

A Silent and a Suffering Savior

Matthew 27:11-14; 24-25; 45-50

> Now Jesus stood before the governor; and the
> governor asked him, "Are you the King of the Jews?"
> Jesus said to him, "You have said so." But when he
> was accused by the chief priests and elders, he made
> no answer. Then Pilate said to him, "Do you not hear
> how many things they testify against you?" But he gave
> him no answer, not even to a single charge; so that the
> governor wondered greatly. ...
>
> So when Pilate saw that he was gaining noth-
> ing, but rather that a riot was beginning, he took water
> and washed his hands before the crowd, saying, "I am
> innocent of this man's blood; see to it yourselves."...
>
> Now from the sixth hour there was darkness
> over all the land until the ninth hour. And about the
> ninth hour Jesus cried with a loud voice, "Eli, Eli, lama
> sabach-tha-ni?" that is, "My God, my God, why hast
> thou forsaken me?" And some of the bystanders hear-
> ing it said, "This man is calling Elijah." And one of
> them at once ran and took a sponge, filled it with vin-
> egar, and put it on a reed, and gave it to him to drink.
> But the others said, "Wait, let us see whether Elijah
> will come to save him." And Jesus cried again with a
> loud voice and yielded up his spirit.

The Passion story as told by Matthew contains a striking
and even shocking emphasis on two things, the eery silence and
the intense suffering of Jesus. Throughout the entire narration of
his trial and crucifixion in the 27th Chapter of Matthew, he speaks
only twice, and in both instances his words are delivered with aus-
tere brevity.

The chief priests and the elders had carefully considered
how to word the charges against Jesus. Knowing that only the

Roman governor, Pontius Pilate, could pronounce a penalty of death by crucifixion, they gave a decided political twist to their primary accusation. They craftily modified Jesus assertion that he was the promised Messiah, into a phrase that appeared hostile to Roman power and supremacy. Jesus had claimed, they said, to be the 'King of the Jews'. Now as he stood before Pilate to be interrogated, the governor directed his questioning to this central charge. "Are you the King of the Jews?" Jesus might have given a lengthy and evasive answer. Instead his reply was not only short, but sharp and biting, "You have said so." After the chief priests and elders had stated all of their accusations, Pilate practically pleaded with Jesus to defend himself. "But he gave no answer, not even to a single charge; so that the governor wondered greatly."

How do we account for the silence of Jesus in this critical time of trial? He was surely capable of defending himself. A short time before, his enemies had tried to trap him into words that could be interpreted as seditious or treasonable. They had inquired of him whether or not it was lawful to pay taxes to Caesar. In answer he asked for a coin and pointing to the picture of Caesar on it, replied, "Render...to Caesar the things that are Caesar's, and to God the things that are God's. And when they heard it, they marveled and left him and went away." (Matt. 22:21) But now he was silent. He gave no answer "not even to a single charge." He spoke not a mumbling word.

It would seem that Jesus simply realized that the time had arrived when words were no longer effective. His enemies were bent upon pressing their charges in the face of all reason or evidence to the contrary. Nothing could deter them now. When Pilate complained that he could find no substance to their accusations, they simply "shouted all the more, "Let him be crucified." There is something to be learned from this strange spectacle of Jesus standing silent before those who were determined to do him grave harm. As the Preacher wrote long ago, "To everything there is a season, and a time to every purpose under the sun."(Ecc. 3:1) There is a time for words and a time to remain quiet, a time to speak and a time to be silent.

There are many occasions when it is far more important to

listen than to talk, so that we learn what others are thinking and when we do speak we have something relevant to say. These are the times when silence is 'golden'. There are other times as at Jesus' trial, when talk is useless and speech is wasted effort. It is vital for us to learn to distinguish clearly when this moment has arrived. Our communication may be limited to a nod of the head, to a plain "yes" or "no" in terms of stating our position. This witness of our bodies and of our lives in the face of hostile opposition which is no longer able or willing to listen to words, takes courage, and a willingness to endure persecution and suffering, possibly even death. But this kind of silent witness is powerful and penetrating. The Scripture says that Pilate "wondered greatly". The Roman governor was impressed, he was captivated by the silence of one who appeared to be innocent of the charges brought against him.

Pilate went through the motions of trying to set Jesus free, but he lacked both conviction and inner strength. The 'governor' was the 'ultimate politician'. The world today is literally filled with his facsimiles. From Europe and Asia to South America and to the legislative halls of our own country the examples of modern day Pilates parade before our eyes on the TV screens. Pilate had no real purpose in life other than the retention of his personal and public power. He knew in his heart what was right, but in the end his only commitment was to do what was most popular, safe and advantageous. The elaborate ritual involved in his 'hand washing' before the crowd, and his whining plea "I am innocent of this man's blood", amounted to little more than pretence. Pilate had the power in his hands to release Jesus or let him be crucified, but his decision would follow a well defined pattern. He would bow to the wishes of those who had the most influence, and let the innocent be damned.

The shallow selfishness and lust for power characterized by Pilate and represented in so many political leaders of our own day, must be confronted and opposed by a sometimes voluble, sometimes silent but always steadfast witness of the Church and its people. It is a witness which the crucifixion of Christ calls us to take up daily on behalf of the innocent, weak and oppressed people of our world.

Unless we have experienced it ourselves, it is difficult to comprehend the feelings of abandonment that drain the hope from the hearts of those in our communities and our world who are deprived of ordinary justice, as Jesus was. These persons are daily denied the respect and dignity due to every human being. They are cast out to the very fringes of our society, to live as best they may. Rejected, forgotten and alone in their helplessness, often homeless and hungry, their plight is most often addressed by those with political power, with a shrug of the shoulders or a spreading of the hands upward, the exact equivalent of Pilate's handwashing ritual.

The Passion story reminds us that Jesus is our Savior precisely because he experienced to its fullness this abandonment. Think of what happened to him during the last few hours of his life. As he agonized over his approaching death and prayed in the Garden of Gethsemane, desperately in need of human companionship, his disciples continually fell asleep. One of his own circle betrayed him into the hands of his enemies for a few coins and identified him with a kiss. One of his closest followers denied that he even knew him. In the hour of his trial all his disciples forsook him and fled. He was slapped and spit on by the chief priests, taunted by the crowds, condemned by the cowardice of the Roman governor, scorned and derided by Pilate's soldiers, and then hung on a cross to die a cruel and lingering death.

No wonder that near the end of his ordeal he literally shouted out his feeling of absolute abandonment, "My God, my God why hast thou forsaken me?"(v. 46) Except for another piercing cry of pain uttered as he died, these are the only words which both Matthew and Mark report that Jesus spoke during the time he hung on the cross. If others were spoken, as we read in Luke and John, then Matthew and Mark chose to emphasize only this single questioning cry of despair. Apparently they believed that it was important to place the stress on Jesus full and complete identification with our humanity. Jesus death was the real thing. What we Christians are most apt to neglect about Jesus is not his divinity, but his humanity. He took upon himself our flesh and blood, with all its limitations, its vulnerability, its pain, its suffering and finally its dying.

Some would say that these words from the Cross are insufficient in themselves, and they even try to explain them away. They point to the fact that the words, "My God, my God, why hast thou forsaken me?" are a direct quotation from the 22nd Psalm, and that Jesus may have been repeating this entire Psalm to himself as an act of prayerful devotion, much as one of us might in a time of grave danger, repeat the 23rd Psalm. We cannot, of course, know for sure. And yet it seems evident to me that in this moment of extremity, these words of Scripture, among the many which he knew from memory, welled up in his mind because he <u>felt</u> them, because he really felt alone, abandoned and forsaken.

From the beginning there have been those who want to water down or deny the full humanity of Jesus, so as not to jeopardize his holiness and godliness. We like a God in the sky rather than a God on the earth. But somehow the humanity of Jesus provides me with the greatest consolation of all. As a result there is a sense in which these words from the Cross, singled out by Matthew and by Mark, have meant more to me than any of the others. This is so because I can identify with them in a way that is not so with some of the other words recorded by Luke and John. I can admire and stand in awe of the one who looks down from the Cross, nails piercing his hands and feet, and with a benevolent smile, prays for his tormentors, "Father, forgive them, for they know no what they do." Yet I know nothing in myself that is capable of that kind of heroism.

But when Jesus cries, "My God, my God, why have you forsaken me?" that I can understand. Here, I can feel his identification with me, and I am grateful for it. Here he speaks as one with my own heart. Here he shares the loneliness, the torment, the pain of my own life.

But is this enough, to have a Savior who shares our life? For me, I think it is. But there is more. The Gospel proclaims to us that God did not in fact forsake Jesus, even though he felt at the time that it was so. In the darkness, the Creator grasped his hand, and walked with him through the valley of the shadow. Our hope is that it will be so for us too!

Easter. The Resurrection of Our Lord

With Fear and Joy

Matthew 28:1-10

> *Now after the sabbath, toward the dawn of the first day of the week, Mary Magdalene and the other Mary went to see the sepulchre. And behold, there was a great earthquake; for an angel of the Lord descended from heaven and came and rolled back the stone, and sat upon it. His appearance was like lightning, and his raiment white as snow. And for fear of him the guards trembled and became like dead men. But the angel said to the women, "Do not be afraid; for I know that you seek Jesus who was crucified. He is not here; for he has risen, as he said. Come, see the place where he lay. Then go quickly and tell his disciples that he has risen from the dead, and behold he is going before you to Galilee; there you will see him. Lo, I have told you." So they departed quickly from the tomb with fear and great joy, and ran to tell his disciples. And behold, Jesus met them and said, "Hail!" And they came up and took hold of his feet and worshiped him. Then Jesus said to them, "Do not be afraid; go and tell my brethren to go to Galilee, and there they will see me."*

The Gospel of Matthew declares that the first witnesses to the resurrection of Jesus were two women, Mary Magdalene and a companion also named Mary. These women and others were among the closest, most loyal and devoted of Jesus followers.

In the grey light of that first Easter dawn these two friends of Jesus walked slowly and sadly toward the tomb where he had been laid. They were heart-broken, and understandably so. They had looked on in horror as the leaders of the religious establishment cried out for the death of the one they loved and revered. They stood in stunned silence as the representatives of a civilized government acquiesced. They had waited by the Cross through the hours of agonized suffering, and numbly watched the broken, bloody corpse of Jesus lowered to the ground and wrapped in a burial sheet. They were disillusioned, discouraged and dejected. And now they were confronted with the ground shaking violently under their feet, with strange sights and sounds in the eerie half-light of this early morning hour.

It's a wonder they had not been paralyzed with fright like the soldiers who had guarded the tomb. It's a wonder they didn't just turn and run. But love and devotion kept their feet moving forward and a messenger of God met them with the words, "Do not be afraid."

The two Marys needed that assurance, and so do we. Fear is a predominant fact of our human existence. From the moment of our birth we experience fear and it never ends until we die. We fear so many things that it is quite impossible to list them all. If each of us were to make our own personal list of the things we fear it would read like a chamber of horrors. We are tormented daily by fear.

Some of us are afraid of the dark, others of high places, or closed places, or open spaces, or of crowds, or of being alone. Name almost any possible condition or situation that we can face in this life, and there will be those among us who react to it with fear. There are fears that are more inclusive and encompassing in nature. Like dragons they guard the entrances to our minds and hearts, and until they are slain or driven away, we remain captive to them. There is the fear of what other people think of us, the fear of being different from others, the fear of being isolated or rejected because of what we think or believe, the fear of those who are different from us, the fear of being laughed at, or rejected or hated.

There are universal fears, which all of us share to one extent or another, and from which there is no real escape. There is the fear of poverty, sickness, suffering, pain, disease, old age, bereavement and death.

When we think of these fears that torment us from within and without, which consume precious energies, paralyze our wills, distort our perception of reality, create uncontrollable panic, drive us into depressions that isolate us from others and rob us of our ability to perform our daily tasks, when we consider fear as a real and ever-present condition of our human life, we may groan inwardly and feel nearly overwhelmed. When Matthew portrays this image of two forlorn and frightened persons, approaching a grave with their hearts filled with fear, it paints a picture of us all.

But the gospel writer goes on to described a more positive and uplifting truth about our lives. In the midst of their gloom and fear, the women are confronted with a word of consolation and encouragement. "Do not be afraid."

On what basis does this messenger of God dare to speak such a word? Is it only a wish, a whistling in the dark? Like the doctor who on diagnosing a fatal disease, tells us not to worry, since it will only make things worse? No, this word of the angel, later repeated by Jesus himself, is based upon something as real and as powerful as our fears.

Much of the fear we feel stems from the fact that a large part of what occurs in our life seems to lie beyond our control and even defies our comprehension. "Our boat is so small, and the sea is so wide." Yet in the face of the utter vulnerability of our humanity we are presented at Easter with a great symbolic truth. It is the essential truth of the resurrection story. Namely, that there are resources of life more powerful than death. There are, in fact, resources that reside within us, available for the asking. We need no longer cringe, dodge, or try to flee from fear. Fear too lies within us. It is a part of ourselves. It is best conquered not by flight, but by recognition, by awareness, and by reliance upon the spiritual power of life and of love. This is the good news of the gospel. The best news that there is. It contains the formula for the amelioration and conquest of the fears that engulf us. As the Scripture says, "Perfect love casts out fear."(I John 4:18)

Since in this life we can never experience love in its absolute perfection, fear continues to cling to us. But now it can be redirected into a force that can at times be a positive factor in our lives. One of the most intriguing passages in Matthew's account of the resurrection is the descriptive phrase he uses regarding the women after they received the message of the angel. "So they departed quickly from the tomb with fear and great joy..."

The fear that had weighed them down was not altogether dissipated, but it was mingled now with joy. It was something altogether different in its effect. Instead of paralyzing them, it invigorated them. It speeded up their hearts and minds and feet. They departed quickly and ran to tell the disciples what had happened.

The Easter message which infuses our fear with joy is not confined to a day of the year or even to the time of crisis. It is a word for all times and all seasons. And once we receive it into our hearts we are impelled to act in new ways, so that its effect is our own experience of resurrection, new life, insight and inspiration. The message given to the two Marys on Easter morning by the angel and by Jesus was essentially the same. "Go quickly and tell the disciples...".(v. 7 & 10) The word to us is the same. "Go quickly and tell." And those of us who have experienced the power of resurrection, the power of God's love in our lives, have, like the two Marys of old, much to tell and to share.

Some of you who read these words have known the sharp pain of emptiness and loneliness. You searched in many places for a remedy to ease it. You sought out pleasures that proved worthless. You drank water from many wells and sipped nectar from many flowers, and wandered down many a blind alley in search of fulfillment. But your hearts remained dissatisfied and sad. Then in some way, by some means you were brought to the awareness of the need for the Spirit of God's love in your life, and you found there a purpose that had eluded you. You discovered an answer to your loneliness and fear in the sharing of that love with others and in the service of your neighbor.

Some of you have marched out in the crusade against injustice and prejudice and oppression, and you felt as if you were crushed and defeated because everything you attempted seemed futile and fruitless, because the world didn't seem to change at all. And then somehow, someway, it became clear, that no act of compassion, no effort in the cause of justice is ever worthless or is ever really defeated. It has its effect and it fulfills a purpose, even when it goes unnoticed by the world. Then you realized that your calling was not necessarily to be successful, but to be faithful, and life took on a new and brighter look. That was resurrection, life in the midst of death. Don't keep these insights to yourself. Go quickly and tell others, so that they too may find encouragement to keep on in the struggle and never give up.

Some of you have endured through long dark nights of pain and suffering. You have known the depths of depression and the choking clutch of despair. You have fallen flat on your face in defeat and no one seemed to care. Then in desperation you cried out to the heavens for help and God somehow brought to you the realization that there was a power within you capable of allaying those fears. That was resurrection. Life in the midst of death. Go quickly and tell others how the power of God's love can deliver them too from the grip of despair.

Yes, whatever God has done for you, whatever part of your fearful life he has filled with joy or peace, go quickly and tell. Go tell it on the mountain. Then your life will become a pulpit from which you sing your alleluias with words, and more important, with deeds that convey the reality and joy of God's love to those who need it most.

2nd Sunday of Easter

Don't Be Afraid of Your Doubts

John 20:19-31

On the evening of that day, the first day of the week, the doors being shut where the disciples were, for fear of the Jews, Jesus came and stood among them and said to them, "Peace be with you." When he had said this, he showed them his hands and his side. Then the disciples were glad when they saw the Lord. Jesus said to them again, "Peace be with you. As the Father has sent me, even so I send you." And when he had said this, he breathed on them, and said to them, "Receive the Holy Spirit. If you forgive the sins of any, they are forgiven; if you retain the sins of any they are retained. "Now Thomas, one of the twelve, called the Twin, was not with them when Jesus came. So the other disciples told him, "We have seen the Lord." But he said to them, "Unless I see in his hands the print of the nails, and place my finger in the mark of the nails, and place my hand in his side, I will not believe. "Eight days later, his disciples were again in the house, and Thomas was with them. The doors were shut, but Jesus came and stood among them, and said, "Peace be with you." Then he said to Thomas, "Put your finger here, and see my hands; and put out your hand, and place it in my side; do not be faithless, but believing." Thomas answered him, "My Lord and my God!" Jesus said to him, "Have you believed because you have seen me? Blessed are those who have not seen and yet believe." Now Jesus did many other signs in the presence of the disciples, which are not written in this book; but these are written that you may believe that Jesus is the Christ, the Son of God, and that believing you may have life in his name.

In the evening of the day of his resurrection Jesus appeared to his disciples as they huddled behind locked doors in fear of the Jewish authorities. Understandably, their gloom was turned into gladness. But one of the disciples, Thomas, was not present when Jesus came. When the others told him they had "seen the Lord", he could not bring himself to believe it. He wanted to see for himself. He insisted, "Unless I see in his hands the print of the nails, and place my finger in the mark of the nails, and place my hand in his side, I will not believe." Thomas is remembered primarily for this expression of unbelief. The diatribe, "doubting Thomas", still describes those who exhibit an attitude of skepticism.

This view of Thomas fails to provide us with the whole picture, for the Bible testifies to the fact that he was not lacking in a certain kind of faith. In the 11th chapter of John we read that when word came concerning the grave illness of Lazarus, Jesus did not immediately go to his friend's aid. The disciples, aware that the religious leaders in Judea were out to kill Jesus, assumed that his hesitancy was based upon prudence. But after two days he surprised them by announcing that he was going to Bethany after all. The disciples protested, "Rabbi, the Jews were but now seeking to stone you, and you are going there again?" When Jesus replied that he was indeed, there must have arisen a question in the minds of some of his followers whether they were willing to risk the danger involved in such a journey. It was Thomas who said to them, "Let us also go, that we may die with him."(John 11:16) Here we see that Thomas had a tenacious and courageous kind of conviction. There were things for which he was willing to die.

Another passage in John's gospel makes it clear that Thomas was quick to question things he could not fully comprehend. On the night before he was crucified, Jesus was trying to prepare his disciples for the shock of his impending death. "Let not your hearts be troubled", he said..."I go and prepare a place for you. I will come again and take you to myself, that where I am there you may be also. And you know the way where I am going." This was too much for Thomas. He could not understand these words and he refused to slide over in silence the questions that welled up in his mind and heart. He interrupted Jesus' comforting words, with a blunt disclaimer and pointed query, "Lord we do not know where you are going; how can we know the way?"(John 14:2-3, 5)

While Thomas may deserve to be dubbed with the title of the "doubter", we must remember that none of the disciples were immune from skepticism. The record of the gospel is that not one of them believed any second-hand testimony concerning the resurrection. They first had to see the risen Lord in person. St. Mark says that when Mary Magdalene told the disciples she had seen Jesus alive, "they would not believe it".(Mark 16:11) Luke records a similar reaction, noting that the witness of the three women who had gone to the tomb and testified that they had seen Jesus there, "seemed to them an idle tale, and they did not believe them."(Luke 24:11) Matthew says that even after the eleven disciples saw Jesus in Galilee following his resurrection, "some doubted."(Mt. 28:17) We must also remember that according to John's record, when Jesus first appeared to the disciples and Thomas was absent, he made a point of showing "them his hands and his side". This was evidently done to help overcome their doubts. It is true that Thomas demanded a more physical and tangible proof than the others, insisting that he would not believe until he actually touched Jesus crucifixion wounds. But in the presence of the Lord, he believed as promptly and completely as the rest. The Scripture does not say that he first reached out and touched Jesus, only that he fell to his knees with a cry of faith, "My Lord and my God." The gentle rebuke which Jesus then administered to Thomas could well have been directed to all of the disciples, "Have you believed because you have seen me? Blessed are those who have not seen and yet believe."(v.29) In effect this word of Jesus applies most of all to those, who like ourselves, are without opportunity to have faith in the resurrection strengthened by sight.

The Scripture says that Thomas was called the "twin", and in a sense we are all twin to Thomas. We are like him because we too have our questions and our doubts. That's why we feel a bit uneasy when we criticize Thomas. We know that in condemning his doubt we condemn our own. In this earthly life, there is no such thing as perfect faith. Doubt is a pervasive ingredient of our humanity. Its scope and intensity vary, but no one escapes it. Those who assert that they believe without question, or boast that they have conquered or outgrown all doubts, may be fooling themselves. One is reminded of couples who after thirty or forty years of marriage claim they have never quarreled or had a serious disagreement. The most charitable thing one can say about this sort of contention is that memory tends also to be imperfect.

Faith is not easy to attain, nor to retain. We are assailed by doubts of every shape and kind. Some of us have intellectual doubts about certain doctrines or creedal formulations, or about such things as the inspiration and factual veracity of the Scriptures. Others have doubts that go far deeper into the affections, and as it were afflict our very heart and soul. We doubt that we can be truly forgiven for wrongs we have done, or the evil in which we have participated. There are times when we question that we really matter at all in the scheme of things, or wonder if life adds up to anything meaningful. We wonder if things do not just happen pretty much by chance, by what we call 'luck' or 'fate'. We have our doubts about the resurrection and the after-life too. What it all adds up to is that we question the very concept of a God who controls or directs our destinies, whose nature is love, and who cares for us as individuals.

In the spite of this universal reality there are those who maintain that in order to be a Christian one must never doubt. It is true that doubts may be dangerous. They can lead to agnosticism and even apathy. They can torment and drive to despair. In this sense it is terrible to have doubts. It would be wonderful to be able to close our eyes and say "I believe" or "I don't believe" and mean it fully and completely. But this is seldom if ever true. In the face of this human reality, perhaps the most dangerous thing we can do is to repress our doubts, to ignore them, to pretend that they have no existence. It may, in fact, be deadly. It can lull us into a false sense of security where we no longer struggle for the faith we need to live. Most of us strive after faith. We want to believe. We are like the centurion who cried out, "Lord, I believe, help my unbelief".(Mk. 9:24) That is our real condition. Like Thomas we remain torn between doubt and belief, between uncertainty and faith. Jesus did not condemn nor reject Thomas. He did not turn away from him. Rather, he came to him in the midst of his unbelief. He accepted his doubts, his searching, his questions. He led Thomas on to the place where some of his doubts were dissolved and some of his questions answered.

As a matter of fact doubt is not so much the opposite of faith as <u>indifference</u>. The "ho-hum" attitude, characterized by the apathetic "yawn" is more deadly dangerous than doubt. Thomas was earnestly searching for faith. That is why he raised his questions. If he hadn't cared, if he had been indifferent, he would never have bothered. The person who reads the Bible and questions some of the things which are read, or listens to a sermon and puzzles over it, may be closer to faith than the person who never bothers to open the Bible, and whose mind is somewhere else when the Word is spoken from the pulpit. When understood in this way doubts can be seen to contain a positive as well as a negative quality. Doubts can become the necessary road along which we travel to a more meaningful faith. Only when we have questioned and tested it, only after we have wrestled with it, as Jacob wrestled with God, only then can we ever hope to claim a faith that is sufficient. We need to encourage and cultivate in our children the questioning mind. The faith that is simply handed down to them by their parents will never be their own until they prove it for themselves. When a young person first begins to question the teachings and the faith passed on to them in the home and Church, they most often discover that their creed was not necessarily false, but that they had really never searched or scratched or struggled to possess it for themselves. That kind of faith, the faith that is real, has to be pounded out on the hard anvil of doubt. It does not come without some sweat and toil and turmoil. Doubt is a part of the anguish involved in the struggle for a personal faith. That is why the poet Tennyson wrote, "There lives more faith in honest doubt, believe me, than in half the creeds."

If you are troubled or bewildered or dismayed by doubts that persist, do not think that Jesus condemns or deserts you anymore than he did Thomas our twin. Rather he continues to come to us in the midst of our doubts. He helps us to act on the faith that we do have. And just as we all have some doubts, so all of us are blessed with some faith. That faith may be small. It may be as tiny as a mustard seed. But Jesus has promised that if we only act on the little faith we have, we can move mountains. It is better to <u>act</u> on a minuscule faith than to sit on a mammoth one! All the questions will never be answered. All the doubts will never be resolved. They keep coming as long as we live. But if we open our hearts, we will find help to act on the convictions we have. Then faith may grow even to that point where we can say with doubting Thomas, "My Lord and My God".

Are You Walking With Me Jesus?

Luke 24:13-35

> That very day two of them were going to a village named Emmaus, about seven miles from Jerusalem, and talking with each other about all these things that had happened. While they were talking and discussing together, Jesus himself drew near and went with them. But their eyes were kept from recognizing him. And he said to them, "What is this conversation which you are holding with each other as you walk?" And they stood still, looking sad. Then one of them, named Cleopas, answered him, "Are you the only visitor to Jerusalem who does not know the things that have happened there in these days?" And he said to them, "What things?" And they said to him, "Concerning Jesus of Nazareth, who was a prophet mighty in deed and word before God and all the people, and how our chief priests and rulers delivered him up to be condemned to death, and crucified him. But we had hoped that he was the one to redeem Israel. Yes, and besides all this, it is now the third day since this happened. Moreover, some women of our company amazed us. They were at the tomb early in the morning and did not find his body; and they came back saying that they had even seen a vision of angels, who said that he was alive. Some of those who were with us went to the tomb, and found it just as the women had said; but him they did not see." And he said them, "O foolish men, and slow of heart to believe all that the prophets have spoken! Was it not necessary that the Christ should suffer these things and enter into his glory?" And beginning with Moses and all the prophets, he interpreted to them in all the scriptures the things concerning himself.

> So they drew near to the village to which they

125

were going. He appeared to be going further, but they constrained him, saying, "Stay with us, for it is toward evening and the day is now far spent." So he went in to stay with them. When he was at table with them, he took the bread and blessed, and broke it, and gave it to them. And their eyes were opened and they recognized him; and he vanished out of their sight. They said to each other, "Did not our hearts burn within us while he talked to us on the road, while he opened to us the scriptures?" And they rose that same hour and returned to Jerusalem; and they found the eleven gathered together and those who were with them, who said, "The Lord has risen indeed, and has appeared to Simon!" Then they told what had happened on the road, and how he was known to them in the breaking of the bread.

It is the afternoon of the first Easter day, and two otherwise unknown followers of Jesus are walking down a lonely country road toward the village of Emmaus, located about seven miles from Jerusalem.

As they stroll along they are involved in animated conversation. They are discussing the momentous events that had taken place in Jerusalem over the past few days. The one in whom they had placed their hopes as the promised Savior had been sentenced to death and then crucified as a common criminal. Now an amazing rumor was circulating. Some women who had visited the tomb where Jesus had been buried, discovered his body was gone, and insisted that he was alive!

Like the rest of the disciples, these two men were not ready to accept their report, without further evidence. They remained disappointed and heartsick over their Lord's death. They wanted to believe the good news, but it seemed impossible. And so they walked down the road with sad faces and battered hopes, expressing to each other their questions, their doubts and perplexities.

And then we read these surprising and striking words: "While they were talking and discussing together, Jesus himself drew near and went with them. But their eyes were kept from recognizing him." Think for a moment about the impact and the meaning of those words on our own lives! What happened to these followers of Jesus is not confined to the distant past or to those particular persons. It happens again and again. It happens to you and to me. In the midst of our troubled lives, our search for meaning, our doubts and perplexities, our loss of hope and our sadness, Jesus himself draws near and walks with us. The good news of the gospel is contained precisely in this affirmation. It proclaims that we have a God and Savior who does not dwell in a place aloof from us, far away, up in the sky, in heaven, or the sweet by and by; but one who comes down to us, walks with us and shares our human life to its fullest. But the tragedy lies in this. When it happens, there is something within us that often keeps us from recognizing it, and as a result we are robbed of its priceless benefits.

So it is important to ask, what was it that kept those two disciples on the road to Emmaus from recognizing that Jesus was walking with them? Above all, I believe it was their lack of expectation. They didn't really believe that Jesus could or would join them there. They were blinded by their doubts. They couldn't experience what they didn't expect. Here was Jesus, the subject of their conversation and their hope, walking with them step by step down that country road, and they didn't even know He was there. Here was the power and presence of God at their elbows, and their eyes were closed to it.

Isn't that true of our own lives as well? Do our hearts and minds fail to perceive the reality of the Lord's presence with us? Maybe we look for and anticipate that presence in special places or on special occasions, on high and holy days, in Church on Sunday, or at the Holy Communion or in the reading of the Bible. Maybe we reach out for it in time of crisis or illness or despair. In desperation we utter our little prayers for help, and find to our surprise, that there is someone there in the darkness to speak a comforting word, to support us in our hour of need!

But what about the ordinary days that fill up by far the larger part of our lives? What about those great gaps of time that exist between the mountain tops of inspiration and the valleys of despair? What about the hours and years that we spend walking along the countless dusty roads of our daily existence? What about all the dull, drab days that are lived out on the flat plain of everyday routine? What about the days when we get up, go to work, fix the meals, take care of the children, pay the bills, go to bed, and rise up to do it all over again?

In his great hymn of the Reformation, "A Mighty Fortress Is Our God", Martin Luther conveyed this very thought in these words, "He's by our side upon the plain, with his good gifts and spirit." That's the real message of Easter and of the entire Gospel. The spirit of Jesus is alive and with us in our world. The presence of God is by our side, on the plain days and the ordinary places, as well as those "far between" high and holy ones. All we need are open hearts and minds full of expectancy.

Can we recognize the presence of Christ with us in the stranger on the street whose smile gives us a needed lift, or in the friend whose timely word of encouragement lifts our spirit just when our hearts are dampened by despair? Can we recognize Jesus walking with us in a fellow worker who befriends us, or in the love of a wife or husband or parent or child? Can we recognize the face of Jesus in the homeless or the sick, the downtrodden, the imprisoned and the oppressed with whom we come in contact? Can we realize that in reaching out to them we receive back a hundredfold? Can we see the Lord walking with us in the flesh and blood of our fellow human beings, or do we miss his presence because we fail to look for it or expect it?

I remember that a painting of the "Road to Emmaus" hung in the home of my grandparents, where I visited often as a child. I recall how comforting it was to me. I didn't know exactly why at the time, but I think it must have been because Jesus appeared to be no different from the other two. He appeared to be just another human being, talking with them, sharing their humble meal. That's the kind of God I could really relate to, and who I knew instinctively, even as a child, could relate to me. Not some distant, far off, other-worldly kind of creature, with halo or wings, but one fully identified with my weakness and my humanity.

Now this awareness of the Lord's presence in the very midst of our life can not only be a great comfort, but a disturbing challenge as well. There are times when we would rather not have the Lord so close to us as the lives of our fellow human beings. There are times when we would prefer to divorce our religion from our daily lives. The challenge is that the presence of God in the lives of others, will never let us off the hook. It will not allow us to close our eyes to the needs of others, or to the injustice which exists at our doorsteps, and which invades our very homes. It is a presence which drives us to strive for the difficult goal which is right, rather than the easy wrong. It is a presence which constantly encourages us to stand for something rather than fall for nothing.

We cannot have our cake and eat it. If we have opened our hearts and minds to the fact of God's presence when we want it and need it, if we recognize that Jesus walks with us, then we must accept the fact that he also challenges us to walk with Him.

Jesus doesn't force the awareness of His presence upon us any more than he did upon those two disciples on the road. But once our eyes are opened to this thrilling truth, then we feel as they did, a fire inside of us, our "hearts burning within". Then we, like those two disciples, are blessed with a new strength to bear our witness to others. Then we are inspired to fight the good fight for justice, and even in the face of discouragement to struggle on with patience and never give up. We can do this, because our courage and our hope is constantly rekindled by the faith that we never walk alone. Jesus is walking with us.

4th Sunday of Easter

A Doorway to Life

John 10:1-10

> *"Truly, truly, I say to you, he who does not enter the sheepfold by the door but climbs in by another way, that man is a thief and a robber; but he who enters by the door is the shepherd of the sheep. To him the gatekeeper opens; the sheep hear his voice, and he calls his own sheep by name and leads them out. When he has brought out all his own, he goes before them, and the sheep follow him, for they know his voice. A stranger they will not follow, but they will flee from him, for they do not know the voice of strangers." This figure Jesus used with them, but they did not understand what he was saying to them.*
>
> *So Jesus again said to them, "Truly, truly, I say to you, I am the door of the sheep. All who came before me are thieves and robbers; but the sheep did not heed them. I am the door; if any one enters by me, he will be saved, and will go in and out and find pasture. The thief comes only to steal and kill and destroy; I came that they may have life, and have it abundantly.*

Jesus referred to himself under many different symbols and figures of speech. In various parts of the gospels he describes himself as light and salt, or as a vine or a shepherd. He did this in order to help people better understand the meaning and purpose of his life and of his mission on earth. In this Gospel text he speaks of himself as the door or the gate through which the sheep enter in and find pasture. The word 'gate' or 'gateway' probably provides a more accurate description of what Jesus had in mind in this picture drawn from the pastoral setting so familiar to those who first listened to his words.

A majority of you who read these words today live among very different surroundings. But we are all familiar with doors and their function. Doors form an entry way. Some doors open up into rooms that are filled with stress and strain, with resentments and rejections, with bitterness and despair. But some doors lead from a cold, cruel, and grasping world into rooms where there is warmth and comfort, the compassion and companionship of those we love. It is this latter kind of entry way that Jesus portrays for us when he says "I am the door." He is a passage-way into a fuller and more meaningful life. As he says in the closing verse of the text, "I came that they may have life, and have it abundantly."(v.10) The key word is "abundantly". It is one thing to live. It is quite another thing to live abundantly. The abundant life is life in its fullest sense. It is life filled with zest and zeal, with compassion and concern. It is the good life, the blessed life.

Jesus says he is like a door which opens into this life. He is not talking here about the entry way from life on earth to life in heaven. Jesus did not just come to provide the doorway to a greater life somewhere else, some other time. We can enter through it into a new and fuller life here and now. We Christians face the constant temptation of turning our faces up to the sky, and our eyes away from the ground upon which we stand. We are constantly encouraged to "keep looking up". We also need to "keep looking down and around" at the realities of this life with which our Creator has blessed us. We can become so enamored of 'eternity' that we literally ignore the world in which we exist. We can become so 'heavenly-minded' that we are of no earthly good!

When Jesus describes himself as a door to abundant life, he does not imply that the threshold into that life can be crossed in an easy or supernatural manner. Access does not come by some magical incantation, by an 'open sesame' formula. It is not actualized through words alone, no matter how persuasively phrased or loudly shouted. We do not pass into the green pastures of abundant living like Alice walking through the 'looking glass' into 'wonderland'. Neither the recitation of a Creed nor the piling up of prayers, nor the pious wishful thinking we sometimes give the name of faith, will grant us passage through this door.

Christ becomes a door through which we enter this new dimension of life only as we follow in his footsteps, only as He becomes the pattern for our living. Discipleship is the key through which the door to abundant life is opened. Jesus came into this world to demonstrate the good life, to be a model of what abundant life is all about. He demonstrated in a very human, down-to-earth manner the reality of this life. He expressed through the here and now of his daily life, its primary components of <u>love</u> and <u>compassion</u> and <u>understanding</u>.

The love that Jesus displayed in his life encompassed all people and all things. It had no exclusionary clauses. It included the publican and the prostitute, the outcasts from society, the thief on the cross, even his enemies. It is normal for us to love those who are bound to us by the ties of kinship. It is natural to love our parents, our spouse, our children, grandchildren, our relatives. In a larger circle we are instinctively drawn to the love of our own countrymen, those of our own race, those who share our convictions and ideals and beliefs. But a love based on any kind of discrimination breeds prejudice. It leads to indifference and even hostility toward those who reside outside this inner circle. The love of Jesus erected no such barriers. It excluded no one. And the true humanity of Jesus means that this love is at least in part possible in our own lives. If we can love our own children and our own family, we can love all young people and all the families of the earth. If we can love the people of our own country or race or religion, then we can love the people of all countries and all races and all religions.

In our text Jesus describes the shepherd as one who truly cares for the sheep and who calls them by name. He lived out this kind of concern. When crowds of people followed him to hear his teaching, Mark wrote "he had compassion on them because they were like sheep without a shepherd."(Mark 6:34) Because he felt in his heart their needs and their hungers, he responded to them. Love fueled by compassion provides us with the energy needed to respond to the needs of others, to their suffering and pain and sorrow. St. Paul wrote, "Rejoice with those who rejoice, weep with those who weep."(Romans 12:15) Compassion is empathy. If we cannot feel with another person's pain as well as their pleasure then we are not truly human, and our love is not complete.

Finally, the compassion of Jesus was rooted in understanding. He took pains to comprehend <u>why</u> people acted in certain ways. He understood what it was that led them to act the way they did. That was why he could look down from the cross on those who had put him there and pray, "Father, forgive them for they know not what they do."(Luke 23:34)

When we become angry with another person, it is important that we try to understand why we are angry, what are the roots of our anger. To understand ourselves is the pathway to peace of mind. In the same way when we have been mistreated or abused it is important that we also try to understand why others have acted in this way. We may discover that the person by whom we have been misused has suffered abuse or been denied a needful love. This is not to say that wrong-doing should be ignored. Discipline or even punishment may be necessary. But when we have really tried to understand the actions of others then it is more likely that we will act in such a way that they, as well as ourselves, receive some real benefit from the experience. Love is not really possible without understanding. To remain unaware and unconcerned about the needs and aspirations and sufferings of others is incompatible with loving them.

It is this love, so clearly revealed in the life of Jesus, a love rooted and grounded in compassion and understanding, which is the gateway to the abundant life. It is the doorway to peace and happiness and joy. It is not easy for any human being to express this love. It takes work and effort. There may be little external reward. It may even result in rejection and persecution and suffering. That is why we need so much the example and inspiration of Jesus. But the inner reward will always be there in abundance, a peace which passes understanding, and a joy which no one can take from us.

The Door is always immediately in front of us, never behind. We only have this day, this moment, to enter. So it is important that we try to express each hour, each day, in some small way, the love which Jesus came to reveal. It may be only a smile to a stranger we pass on the street, or a word of encouragement or sympathy to someone who needs it. It might be the simplest act of caring for God's creation, watering a flower, or planting a tree, or refusing to use poisonous pesticides. It might be almost any conceivable act of love, no matter how minute. Doing little things, and doing them now, is important. Never underestimate their value. They are like a stone tossed into the water. They have a rippling effect. They spread out and their example can influence others in ways we cannot even imagine. What is just as important, they can bring peace to our heart and liberation to our soul. They can carry us through the doorway to Life.

The Call To Do Great Things

John 14:1-12

> *"Let not your hearts be troubled; believe in God, believe also in me. In my Father's house are many rooms; if it were not so, would I have told you that I go to prepare a place for you? And when I go and prepare a place for you, I will come again and will take you to myself, that where I am you may be also. And you know the way where I am going." Thomas said to him, "Lord, we do not know where you are going; how can we know the way?" Jesus said to him, "I am the way, and the truth, and the life; no one comes to the Father, but by me. If you had known me, you would have known my Father also; henceforth you know him and have seen him."*
>
> *Philip said to him, "Lord, show us the Father, and we shall be satisfied." Jesus said to him, "Have I been with you so long, and yet you do not know me, Philip? He who has seen me has seen the Father; how can you say, 'Show us the Father'? Do you not believe that I am in the Father and the Father in me? The words that I say to you I do not speak on my own authority; but the Father who dwells in me does his works. Believe me that I am in the Father and the Father in me; or else believe me for the sake of the works themselves." "Truly, truly, I say to you, he who believes in me will also do the works that I do; and greater works than these will he do, because I go to the Father."*

On the night before he died, Jesus shared a last supper with his disciples. After they had eaten, he took a towel and proceeded to wash their feet. When Peter protested Jesus explained the meaning of this act. Just as he was willing to serve them, even to the point of laying down his life, so their discipleship was to be expressed in service and love to one another and to all people. Then he began to prepare them for the sudden separation of his approaching death. He knew that in their bereavement they would be distraught and dismayed. In these opening verses of the 14th chapter of John, Jesus speaks words of comfort, encouragement and empowerment to his frightened and bewildered disciples. He tells them not to be afraid but to simply believe and trust in God and in his own promise that their separation will not be permanent. The first six verses of this chapter are appointed to be read at funeral services, and they are most often interpreted as relating only to the after-life.

But in this entire passage, as in the whole of the New Testament, the basic theme is not life after death, but life before death, life here in this world. As the Scriptures repeatedly affirm, eternal life begins now, "this is eternal life, that they know thee the only true God, and Jesus Christ whom thou has sent."(John 17:3), "God gave us eternal life and this life is in his Son. He who has the Son has life."(I John 5:12) So we need to look again at this familiar 'funeral' passage, and view it in the light of the comfort it provides for our daily life in the world.

"In my Father's house are many rooms, or resting places... and when I go and prepare a place for you, I will come again and will take you to myself that where I am there you may be also." The Father's house is not confined to some shadowy heavenly realm. God created this earth. This world is our house, with its many rooms, over which the Lord rules and reigns. It is for this reason that our hearts should not be troubled or sad, for God is here with us and in control. As a well known hymn puts it "This is my Father's world, O let me not forget, that though the wrong seems oft so strong, God is the ruler yet! This is my Father's world; why should my heart be sad?"

In this world the Father provides, and Jesus himself prepares resting places, rooms, where pilgrims, worn and battered by the troubles and the struggles of this life, can find renewed strength and refreshment as they are united again with the living spirit of the Christ. But the disciples are hard pressed to comprehend the meaning of Jesus words. Jesus has spoken in abstract and even mystical terms. Thomas, the realist, is the first to give voice to his questions. Jesus tells Thomas that to know and see him is to know and see the Father. Now Philip is perplexed, "Lord," he says "show us the Father and we shall be satisfied." At this point Jesus appears to realize that words and concepts are not enough to explain the reality of God and of his own intimate relationship with God. So he says to Philip, "Believe me that I am in the Father and the Father in me," or (if that's impossible to comprehend) then "believe me for the sake of the works themselves."

There we have it! What impels us to accept Jesus claim to be the Son of God in a special and unique way, is not the claim in itself. What convinces us is not what Jesus said but what he did. What persuades our hearts to believe that he is the Way and the Truth and the Life are his works of love and healing, of reconciliation and sacrificial giving. If the New Testament recorded only the words of Jesus, and of his claim to be the Son of God, I must confess that I would read it with interest but without conviction, and with many questions left unanswered. It is the life of Jesus that persuades me he was someone more than special. It is those works of amazing love which I can only describe as "God-like", that lead me, in turn, to trust in his words.

But having said this I am then confronted in the final words of this Scripture passage with an incredible promise! For here Jesus says, "Truly truly I say to you, he who believes in me will also do the works that I do; and greater works than these will he do, because I go to the Father." Can this possibly be true, that people like you and me can continue the very work of Jesus here on earth, and even surpass what he did? It would be easy to simply smile at these words and pass them by. But Jesus surely meant what he said.

Jesus left this world a different place than it was when he came. He brought into it a kind of love and compassion that changed the lives of those he touched and gave them new hope and courage and concern for others. Then Jesus left this world in order to prepare, to 'make room', for his followers to carry on his work, and to expand it.

Jesus ministry was limited in time. It lasted perhaps little more than a single year, at the most, three. His ministry was limited in scope. His world was small in terms of its geography, and he purposely confined his activities pretty much to his own nation and his own people. His plan was primarily to teach and train and inspire a small cadre of disciples who would amplify and extend his message and the lifestyle he exemplified into all the world. That is the continuing task which Jesus has placed into our hands, and it is a great one.

The words of the Psalmist are all together true; as it is written, "The Lord has done great things for us."(Ps.126:3) And what follows is that we are called to do great things for the Lord, in our time and in our day. There is even more to be done than in Jesus day. There are more people in need, but there are more resources to utilize, more knowledge to employ. Our scientific knowledge has increased to the point where we can do amazing things. We have learned how to heal diseases, transplant organs and prolong life. We have learned to increase the production of food to the point where there could be enough for all. We have learned how to cleanse the air and the waters of the earth of harmful waste and pollution. We have learned through a sad and prolonged experience the futility and waste of the cold war and the agony of real war. We are at the point where we can do those "greater things" the Lord has promised we are able to do. The critical question that remains is, will we take Jesus at his word, and set our hearts and minds and hands and feet to that great task?

There is no question that we have the means to do greater things in our day than in the time that Jesus walked this earth. But this very capacity for doing good also contains the potential of doing evil. The power to sustain life can be misused if it is simply used to prolong the time of one's suffering, or if it is utilized only on behalf of the powerful and the wealthy. So it is with every area of our life. Only when our amplified ability and our increased knowledge is inspired and directed by the Spirit and example of Jesus, will these "greater things" become a reality.

Each one of us has a witness to bear if that goal is to be accomplished. In other words, each of us has an individual contribution to make, however small, toward the realization of the "greater things' that Jesus envisioned. And this witness, in order to be effective, must be, as was the case with Jesus, primarily in terms of our actions rather than our words alone. There are times when our words can be 'acts'. If they are spoken truthfully and courageously and appropriately. If they are spoken when needed and are backed up by our deeds. But talk for talk's sake, talk that is unrelated to one's acts, is not only cheap, but worthless. That is why people are becoming more and more turned off by the ceaseless 'talk' of politicians.

One of the characters on the T.V. show, "Saturday Night Live" once did an impression of George Bush in which he says "I'm just talking now, not saying anything." Slightly altered, those words are a description of too much of what goes by the name of a 'Christian witness,' just talking, not really doing anything.

If we would really say something to our world in that little corner where we live and work, that would push it even an iota of an inch in the direction of those "greater things" the Lord has envisioned, then we must be saying to others as Jesus once said to his questioning disciples, "Believe me for the sake of the works themselves."

Putting Love to the Test

John 14:15-21

> *"If you love me, you will keep my commandments. And I will pray the Father, and he will give you another Counselor, to be with you for ever, even the Spirit of truth, whom the world cannot receive, because it neither sees him nor knows him; you know him, for he dwells with you, and will be in you.*
>
> *I will not leave you desolate; I will come to you. Yet a little while, and the world will see me no more, but you will see me; because I live, you will live also. In that day you will know that I am in my Father, and you in me, and I in you. He who has my commandments and keeps them, he it is who loves me; and he who loves me will be loved by my Father, and I will love him and manifest myself to him."*

This entire chapter of John's Gospel is centered in Jesus' words of comfort and encouragement directed to the fear and anxiety in the hearts of his disciples as they face the prospect of his approaching death.

Jesus assures them that he will never abandon them, never leave them as orphans alone and unaided in a world filled with evil. They may not be able to see him any longer, but he will come to them and abide with them in the form of the Spirit.

This is wonderful good news. It is for us as well as those first disciples. It is a promise we need. But the abiding presence which Jesus promises is not designed nor intended to bring only a personal sense of inner security. The Spirit through which Jesus comes to us and dwells within us, is the Spirit of Truth, and the spirit of Love. It's purpose is not just to keep us safe and secure from harm, but to provide us with the strength to serve and the courage to care. It's purpose is to fill us with a driving love for the truth and with an earnest desire to keep the commandments of Jesus to the best of our ability.

Jesus tells us, that there is a sure way to test whether or not we have really received His spirit into our hearts and lives. "If you love me", he says, "you will keep my commandments."(v.15) and again, "They who have my commandments and keep them are those who love me."(v.21) When we love Jesus enough to do this, that is our assurance that his spirit dwells in us. "In that day you will <u>know</u> that I am in the Father, and you in me, and I in you." (v.20) That blessed assurance stems directly from the 'down-to-earth' reality that we keep the commandments of Jesus, not perfectly of course, but persistently, prayerfully, and to the best of our ability.

And what are these commandments? Jesus summed them up for us in a very concise way. Love God with all your heart and soul and mind and strength and love your neighbor as yourself.(Mark 12:30-31) These two commandments are actually one and the same, since we can only love God in and through our neighbor. As we read in the 1st Epistle of John "If anyone says, I love God and hates his brother, he is a liar; for he who does not love his brother whom he has seen, cannot love God, whom he has not seen."(I John 4:20) In the same way to love Jesus really means to love each other. Jesus himself put it this way, "As you did it to one of the least of these my brethren, you did it to me." (Matt. 25:40)

So the crucial test of whether or not the spirit of Jesus' dwells in us, is the 'down-to-earth' love that we express for our fellow human beings in this world. If we fail to apply this test, or take it for granted or ignore it, we deceive ourselves and the truth is not in us.

It is because this test is so often disregarded, that much of what we hear and see and call 'religion' or 'Christianity' misses the mark. If we can boast to others of how strongly we believe, or how wonderful it is to have faith in God, and yet remain opposed to the racial integration of our neighborhoods and schools, and to special efforts to uplift and support those who live in poverty and oppression, then our claims remain hollow and meaningless. If we can point to the day and the hour when we were 'born again', if we can speak in tongues, but continue to reject and isolate ourselves from those who act or think or look differently from ourselves,

144

then the claim becomes suspect, and our speaking only a 'babble'. If we can give verbal testimony and witness to our faith in Christ, if we can be 'evangelists', and invite others to our church, but continue to manipulate, control and dominate them, to express selfishness and paternalism rather than compassion and concern, then our credentials are without substance and lack authority.

If we read the Bible every day, and pray before every meal and go to church every Sunday and contribute generously, but slander our brothers and sisters, rip them apart behind their backs, tear them down rather than build them up, then all of our reading and praying and worshipping amounts to nothing because it has nothing to do with the Spirit of Jesus. In this same vein St. Paul wrote, "If I speak in the tongues of men and angels, but have not love I am a noisy gong or a clanging symbol... and if I have all faith, so as to remove mountains, but have not love, I am nothing. If I give away all I have... but have not love, I gain nothing.(I Cor. 13:1-3) There is a direct and vital connection between possessing the spirit of Jesus and expressing the love of Jesus.

We are to "test the spirits to see whether they are from God" (I John 4:1), for "the fruit of the spirit is Love, joy, peace, patience, kindness, goodness, faithfulness, gentleness, self-control."(Gal. 5:22) If those fruits are not evident in our lives then we know that the spirit of Jesus is absent too. Love is always the test of the spirit. As we sing in the hymn "They will know we are Christians by our love." And this love, which is the true mark of the spirit's presence is never just a detached feeling of well-being or inner peace. It involves discipleship, cross-bearing, and servanthood. It is a love whose shape and form is always molded by the example of Jesus.

Once we understand and accept this then we are able to define and pin-point some of its specific ingredients. It is important to do this, in order that our conception of love never remains dim and hazy, but takes on a definite definition. If we look carefully at Jesus' life, we cannot help but note that a basic ingredient of his love was the simple yet profound acceptance of our humanity. The love of Jesus never insisted that we go a certain way in our life. "If you love me," he said, "keep my commandments." He stood ready to assist, to encourage, to enhance the lives of his disciples but never dictated what they had to do. His love is encompassed in the Christ figure portrayed in the Apocalypse, "Behold I stand at the door and knock. If anyone hears my voice and opens the door, I will come in..." (Rev.3:20) Here lies a definite and vital characteristic of Christian love. It stands ready to assist, but does not seek to control.

So many times when we attempt to aid or advise others, we tend to point them more or less forcefully in the direction we desire. But how much more valuable it would be to assist them to explore their own interests and ideas and potentialities. This principle not only has relevance for our personal relationships but contains important social implications as well. It means that we allow our humanitarian and charitable efforts to be directed more by the needs and desires of those we wish to help than by our own. This may appear to be a simple matter of using plain common sense. Yet it is amazing how often it is ignored. Two examples come to mind. It is often true that when school officials develop plans to raise the educational standards and strategies of teaching so as to provide students with a better education, the only persons who are not consulted or involved in the actual construction of the plan are the students themselves. When state officials draw up new legislation that would improve the 'welfare system', people on welfare are seldom given a role in the process. We should have learned this 'lesson of love' through the costly mistakes we have made in seeking to provide assistance to 'minority' groups in this country and 'foreign aid' programs designed to help those in other lands by agencies like the World Bank and the International Monetary Fund.

One of the most vital principles to follow in any 'aid' program is to listen carefully to the ideas and expressed needs of those who are the recipients of the support and to never do for people what they are able to do for themselves. If Christians and the Church at large are to express the love of Christ in a tangible way they should lead the way in the development of programs which assist people to respond in their own way to their own problems.

Nothing expresses more explicitly the complete acceptance of our humanity contained in the love of Jesus than his own incarnation. Though he was in the form of God, he humbled himself and took upon himself our flesh and blood. He experienced to its fullest our temptations, frustrations, our sorrows and joys, our pain and our pleasures, our suffering and our death. He walked where we walk, and felt what we feel. That's what it means, as Martin Luther King, Jr. put it, "to love somebody". It means to walk in their shoes. That is a vital part of what St. Paul calls "genuine love", to "rejoice with those who rejoice and to weep with those who weep".(Romans 12:9,15)

If our attempts to help someone along the way is based on anything less than a full identification with the humanity we share, then it is less than real love, for it is less than the love with which Christ loves us. We must not be afraid to put our love to the test. Does it measure up? Does it express something of the <u>acceptance</u> contained in Jesus love? Only in this way can we know whether we have opened our hearts to the Spirit of Christ, whether his spirit dwells in us.

7th Sunday of Easter

In and To the World

John 17:1-11

>*When Jesus had spoken these words, he lifted up his eyes to heaven and said, "Father, the hour has come; glorify thy Son that the Son may glorify thee, since thou hast given him power over all flesh, to give eternal life to all whom thou hast given him. And this is eternal life, that they know thee the only true God, and Jesus Christ whom thou hast sent. I glorified thee on earth, having accomplished the work which thou gavest me to do; and now, Father, glorify thou me in thy own presence with the glory which I had with thee before the world was made.*
>
>*I have manifested thy name to the men whom thou gavest me out of the world; thine they were, and thou gavest them to me, and they have kept thy word. Now they know that everything that thou hast given me is from thee; for I have given them the words which thou gavest me, and they have received them and know in truth that I came from thee; and they have believed that thou didst send me. I am praying for them; I am not praying for the world but for those whom thou hast given me, for they are thine; all mine are thine, and thine are mine, and I am glorified in them. And now I am no more in the world, but they are in the world, and I am coming to thee."*

During the trial of Jesus, he was brought before the Roman governor for questioning. Pilate asked him if he had really claimed, as his accusers asserted, that he was the "King of the Jews"? Jesus had answered, "My kingship is not of this world, if my kingship were of this world, my servants would fight, that I might not be handed over to the Jews, but my kingship is not from the world."(John 18:33-36)

149

Pilate was shrewd enough to grasp that this answer did not represent an outright denial of the chief priests accusation: "So you are a king?" he asked. Jesus' answer, "You say that I am a king", is not, as often interpreted, evasive. It is best translated as a simple, "Yes, you are right, I am a king." And He proceeds immediately to explain in what sense this is so. "For this I was born, and for this I have come into the world, to bear witness to the truth."(John 18:37)

It is against this background, this description of a kingdom and mission which is not of the world, or from the world, but in the world and to the world, that Jesus' farewell prayer, recorded in this text, must be understood.

He prays that the disciples, who will be left alone, following his death, may be strengthened to bear a continuing witness to the truth he had come to reveal. Jesus will no longer be in the world to lead and guide and inspire them with his physical, human presence, but the disciples will remain in the world.(v.11) In the words of this same prayer which continues on following the text, he makes a clear connection between his own kingship and mission and that of his disciples. "They are not of the world," he says, "even as I am not of the world. I do not pray that thou shouldst take them out of the world, but that thou shouldst keep them from the evil one." And then he adds, "As thou didst send me into the world, so I have sent them into the world."(John 17:16,18) The identification with his own Incarnation is here made complete. Just as it was necessary in order for Jesus to fulfill God's purpose that He take on human flesh and blood and come down into the world, so this world is always and forever to be the sphere where God's work is to be done through the lives of the faithful. It is the place where the ongoing witness to the truth is to take place. This is precisely what lends urgency to the temporal and 'worldly' aspect of the Christian life and faith, and to the daily, faithful performance of our earthly tasks.

The tendency to place more importance on the world to come than this world, upon eternity rather than the present moment, represents a violation of the Biblical witness. It diverts our attention from the basic concerns to which Jesus constantly directed his disciples. We are faced always with the temptation to lift our eyes up and away from the world, to the more tranquil and halcyon realm above. We are tempted to view religion in a kind of mystical fashion, as a way to evade or escape the troubles of the world. There is no question but that this formulation of the faith affords needed solace and comfort. The problem is that it ignores the earnest, heartfelt prayer of Jesus as recorded in this text. It is a prayer beseeching God to give his disciples strength and courage to carry on the work he began <u>in</u> and <u>to</u> the world, the work of witnessing to the truth.

The truth to which Jesus calls us to witness, is simple but hard. It is the truth that this is God's earth, and we are to care for it with loving concern. It is the truth that we are all the children of God, and that we are to love one another and treat one another with respect and compassion and understanding. It is the truth that those with the most pressing needs are to be given priority in terms of our limited energies and resources. It is the truth that our task is not so much to help those in need as to provide for them the opportunity to help themselves.

When we confront the task of relating these Gospel truths to the concrete problems of the world, we see just why Jesus prayed that we would be given needed strength. Caring for the environment, working for social justice, for peace, for the poor and the oppressed, is difficult work. It is both complicated and controversial, and we would prefer a religion that avoids both complexity and contention. No wonder Jesus prayed that his disciples be kept from the "evil one".(John 17:15)

We often hear it said that the Church and its ministers should proclaim the Gospel and stay out of politics. But that constitutes an impossible demand. If one does not relate the Gospel to politics, then the Gospel is not being preached. The essence of the Gospel lies in its witness to truth in our earthly life, and politics affects every aspect of that life and influences it for good or ill.

The real question is not "Should the Church and its people stay out of politics? The real question is how and in what way should their convictions be related to the political. The fact that there is no easy answer to that question does not excuse us from the effort to find one. We are called to witness to the truth. It must be registered in terms of a voice and a vote for peace and understanding, for the acceptance of all people, for human rights and human dignity, for social justice, for the care, support and encouragement of the poor, the oppressed, the outcast and the rejected, and for the care of the earth.

Certainly Christians will not always agree on how this is to be done, particularly with regard to the specifics. If, however, we approach these crucial matters in the Spirit of Jesus and in accord with his prayer, we may find to our surprise that we agree more often than not. There will always be controversy, but conflict can lead not only to division, but to deeper understanding. It is true that Jesus wants his followers to be united in their efforts. He wants us to work together. So in the last words of this text he prays to God, "that they may be one, even as we are one."(17:11) That prayer motivates us to seek sincerely for Christian unity. Still it would be contrary to Jesus earlier words to pursue unity at the expense of truth.

We are often told that involvement in the political aspects of life is the chief cause of division among Christians. That charge is open to question. Through the years churches have experienced tremendous discord over doctrinal differences. Wars have been waged over minor theological distinctions, and these kinds of innocuous clashes continue to plague Christians today. Once we realize that the deepest confession of faith and witness to truth lies in the loving service of the earth and of all living things, there will be more concentration on the practical aspects of living out our religious convictions. Here disagreements will exist, but they have more chance of resolution. The unity that Jesus prayed for may well be realized, not so much by doctrinal consensus as in the cross-denominational quest for justice and in the service of suffering humanity. Jesus reminded us that it is not enough to say "Lord, Lord". What is required is the doing of God's will.(Matt:7:21) By seeking for a unity based on faith active in love and justice, Christians can contribute not just to their own concord but to the oneness of the world they have been called to love and to redeem. They can carry their witness for peace and harmony in and to the world.

152